When God Stepped In: A Collection of True Stories

Nick Nichols

Published by Nick Nichols, 2023.

While every precaution has been taken in the preparation of this book, the publisher assumes no responsibility for errors or omissions, or for damages resulting from the use of the information contained herein.

WHEN GOD STEPPED IN: A COLLECTION OF TRUE STORIES

First edition. May 29, 2023.

Copyright © 2023 Nick Nichols.

ISBN: 979-8223407508

Written by Nick Nichols.

Table of Contents

I dedicate this book to the Lord Jesus Christ who makes all things new!...and who made my life profoundly new on February 2, 1971. Without Jesus, there would be absolutely no stories to tell.

~~~

"For God so loved the world that he gave his one and only Son, that whoever believes in him shall not perish but have eternal life." --John 3:16 (NIV)

~~~

I also dedicate this book to our adult children Holly, Heather, Christian, Brittany, and our three unborn children in heaven, Jonathan, Jessie, and Jordan.

~~~

Lastly, this book is dedicated to Barb, my lovely wife of forty-five years, without whom the reader would have a more difficult time understanding what I wrote. God knew best and married me to a live-in grammarian who rescued me from dangling participles, split infinitives, comma splices and the dreaded squinting modifiers!
~~~

God's Roadside Service

CLUNK!! Now sitting with the back half my car on the road and the front half of my car with its wheels dangling in the air over a large three-foot deep utility ditch—I felt stupid! It was dark at 2 AM in the morning, and I hadn't seen the newly cut ditch as I turned into our townhouse complex. I was really tired, and I mumbled half to myself and half to the Lord, "I can't believe I just did that!"

It looked like the utility company had taken a knife and sliced off the side of the road. The pavement had a clean cut and sharp edge that dropped off into the ditch. Thankfully, the road was empty with traffic so there wasn't any danger to myself or anyone else. I thought about getting some concrete blocks and a jack and trying to jack the front end of my car back up onto the pavement. But I was so tired, and my thought didn't immediately transfer into action.

My car was angled down with my headlights lighting up the dirt and loose drainage tiles lying in the ditch. Suddenly out of the dark, three strong-looking young men walked into the light of my headlights from three different directions arriving at the same moment. Because the angle of my car was pointing down and with the dark tinting in the top of my windshield, I could only see these guys from the chest down.

At the same time, one grabbed the front of my car, one grabbed the left front, one grabbed the right front, and in unison, they lifted my car into the air and rolled it back on the pavement. It was an old car, and I was frantically trying to crank my window down to thank these guys, but by the time I got the window down—they were gone!

It all happened in a matter of minutes from the time I drove off the road. I was so amazed at what had just taken place that I just sat there wondering if they were angels!! I prayed, "Lord, I don't know if those were angels or not, and I don't know why I never saw their faces, but thank you Lord, thank you so much for lifting me out of the ditch."

I backed my car up, made the turn into our complex, and drove to our townhouse; exhausted, I climbed into bed, and still in a state of marvel, whispered, "Thanks again Lord for your roadside service," and fell fast asleep.

"But the LORD looks with favor on those who respect him. He watches over those who put their hope in his faithful love." Psalm 33:18 —(NIRV)

Why God Gave Us Memory

Hidden behind the rows of musty smelling old books, I sat at a study desk . . . weeping.

I was angry and depressed. I thought to myself, "Where is God when I need Him the most!" I was in total despair. My problem was too big and carried with it too much pain. I was trying to trust God for the answer, but there I sat hidden among the books on the thirteenth floor of the university library . . . alone, with no answer.

Staring at the floor, I noticed an old book on the bottom shelf, and though surrounded by thousands of old books, this book caught my attention. Kneeling, I carefully slid out the small book with its fragile binding. Curious at how old it really was, I checked to see when it was published; it was old—a book from 1830! It appeared to be a book of essays. As I sat back down at my desk, the book fell open to the beginning of one of the essays titled, "Why God Gave Us Memory."

The author stated that God gave us memory so when we are in the middle of a problem in our life, we can look back and remember how God had helped us in the past, and what He has done in the past,

He will again do for us in the future. Immediately, the profound truth of this simple statement stopped my overwhelming despair dead in its tracks. I quietly prayed through tears, "Father, you have clearly spoken to me. Help me to trust you. I am so sorry I doubted and complained. Please forgive me. In the name of Jesus, Amen."

Wiping the tears from my eyes, I sat back and began to "remember." Back when I was getting ready to go to college, I needed a car. My parents couldn't afford to buy me one, and I didn't have enough money, so I began praying for a car. When it was near time to leave for school, out of the blue, my uncle Warnie gave me his old car. He was trading up, but couldn't get what he wanted for the trade-in, so he gave it to me.

Then I recalled the time I needed gas money to go help a friend but had none. Not even a nickel. I prayed, "Lord, this friend really needs help tonight, and I don't have any money to buy gas. Please help me! In the name of Jesus, Amen." That day in the mail I received a forgotten tax return that was post marked six months earlier! Apparently, it had been lost in the mail trying to follow my move from Canada. I cashed the check and drove down that night to help my friend.

The memories kept coming...Another time I was walking through a large public building and was very hungry and didn't have any money. I kind of muttered under my breath, "Lord, I'm really hungry." A couple of minutes later, a man walks up to me carrying a large brown sack. He says, "We just had a luncheon upstairs, and I didn't want to see all these good roast beef sandwiches thrown out . . . would you like one?" I think my dropped jaw and the shocked look on my face shouted "YES!" loud and clear as he handed me the huge sandwich. As I was eating, all I could think was, "Wow, Lord! You make a GREAT roast beef sandwich!"

More memories kept flooding my mind, and all I could do was weep and smile. Finally, sitting up and again wiping the tears from my eyes, I had "remembered" and was filled with peace and confidence. What He had done in the past, He would do again . . . and solve my difficult problem.

Postscript: He did.

I will remember the deeds of the Lord; yes, I will remember your miracles of long ago. –Psalms 77:11 (NIV)

Say One Word and Die

POP, POP, POP! Johnnie barely heard the sounds above the noise of the engine as he roared 90-miles-an-hour on a short straightaway in the back hills of Kentucky. A noise exploded behind him as his back passenger window was shot out. Johnnie was a Moonshine "Runner" back in the 1940s, hauling illegal whiskey called Shine, for short, to distributors. He had just picked up a load of Shine made by the bootleggers and was on his way to cash in on the haul.

POP, POP, POP! Now he was positive the police ambush along the road was trying to shoot out his engine! Shine was big business and his load was worth a bundle! What the police didn't know was that Johnnie had put his mechanic skills to good use by moving his engine block to the back of his large sedan on a shortened rear drive shaft. Under the hood was where his jugs of Shine were now "safely" stowed away, and if they didn't shoot out all the jugs, some Shine would still make it, and if the police couldn't stop him, he would stay out of prison and get his money—so down the road he roared.

There's a saying back in the hills that Shine only comes in two flavors, "legal" and "illegal." Tax evasion was the name of the game, which became a deadly game. The bootleggers, who made the Shine along with the Runners, were in big demand—the government wanted them for tax evasion, the police wanted them for breaking all kinds of laws, and organized crime wanted them to join them. Because there was so much money to be made, a lot of people ended up either in prison or dead.

Into that world in the early 40s walked a skinny new preacher with fiery red hair with a wife and infant son. Reverend David Irvine had a love for the folks in the hills of Kentucky despite their choice of livelihood. However, it soon became clear that these folks "don't trust no outsiders." It took some time before David and Dorothea his wife won the right to be part of the veiled community. As months passed, little by little, he was able to share with them how Jesus loved them, but probably more important was not what he said, but what he did—the way the Reverend and his wife cared for the folks' spiritual and physical needs translated into a love that the hill folks could see and understand.

In time, some made the decision to trade in their life of bootleg crime for new life in Christ. It was no small decision—these were folks whose families had been bootleggers for generations, brewing and selling the illegal Shine and making good money in the process...as long as they managed to live through the gunfire. The new bootleg-believers changed their ways by quitting the business and began making a legal living. They were happy, honest people now, but their friends that were still making Shine, were NOT happy and NOT honest and saw these new bootleg-believers as a threat to their livelihood! But the real source of the problem, as they saw it, was that red-headed skinny preacher who had moved into their territory with his God-message!!

The angry bootleggers devised a plan to take care of the source of the problem and saw their opportunity one Sunday evening. David had been invited to speak at a small church that was so remote he had to drive up a dry riverbed covered with smooth water-worn rocks to get there. Once there, he parked his car, and he along with his wife and infant son made their way to the church through the woods in the twilight of the setting sun. After speaking, some men came to him and said they had heard that some bootleggers from another county had come to stone him to death in the riverbed where he was parked. David turned to his wife and calmly said, "Follow me to the car, and don't say a word to anyone."

Carrying a lantern, the young preacher and his small family made their way back through the dark woods to the car, and sure enough, just as the men had warned . . . as they stepped out into the riverbed clearing, by the glow of the lantern, they saw the group of rough, tough, mean-looking men standing near their car. They were glaring at David with hatred in their eyes and big stones in their hands. David breathed a silent but serious prayer, "Jesus, if we live or die, we are yours, and if you want us to live, then protect us from these men."

David walked to his car and saw the doors had been wired shut to prevent a quick escape. Not looking again at the men and with his wife and infant son beside him, he handed the lantern to his wife and unraveled the stiff rusty wire from the handles. Opening the front passenger door, he helped his wife and baby inside, got in the driver's side and slowly drove back down the dry riverbed safely disappearing into the night.

No stones. No killing. Only protection.

A few days later, he was approached by some local men who said, "David, we know those men that were waiting by your car, and if you had said one word to them, they would have stoned you to death."

With a heart full of gratitude, David silently prayed, "Thank you, Jesus . . . for making sure we didn't say one word!"

"If we live, we live to honor the Lord. If we die, we die to honor the Lord. So whether we live or die, we belong to the Lord." —-Romans 14:8 (ISV)

Postscript: The now deceased Reverend David Irvine was my father-in-law and the infant in the story is my brother-in-law, David. I would like to thank Betty Ann (his daughter) and Carol (his daughter-in-law) for their input about the story. Most of it I had remembered from Dad Irvine telling me himself about the near stoning, the Lord's delivery, and the wonderful times of ministry he had in the back woods of Kentucky as a young preacher.

God preserved David's life on that day, and his small family of one son grew to a larger family of three sons and two daughters—a family that continued to experience the Lord's ongoing faithfulness. Of Scottish descent, David's parents were the first in his family to come to America from the old country, and David was the first in his family line to accept God's gift of salvation through Jesus—David's example of being a Christ follower continues to this day in the lives of his children, grandchildren, and great grandchildren. May his legacy continue.

God Spoke, and I Looked in the Bushes!

I will never forget The Voice. Climbing up the steep steps to my college library that cold December morning, my thoughts were on the paper I needed to do research for. The library was just opening, and I was alone on the steps. Suddenly my ears are jarred by this very loud and authoritative voice! "I want you to go to Canadian Bible College this coming semester and for the following year." It was so loud I thought my friends might be playing a joke on me, so I glanced behind the tall bushes by the steps. As I looked, my heart was telling me I had just heard God, the Creator of the Universe, verbally speak to me! Almost like Moses with some doubting at the burning bush I said, "But Lord . .

. Nobody applies to go to another college in two weeks' time!!" He was silent, and I got the message.

It was two weeks before the end of the semester and Christmas break at my upstate New York college. The only thing I knew about Canadian Bible College was that my roommate had a brochure lying on his desk from them. I had never heard of the school before and didn't even know where it was located in Canada. The memory of The Voice compelled me onward, and I asked my roommate if I could have the brochure with its attached response card. I filled in my name, home address, and said, "Here goes Lord," and dropped it in the mail.

The school I discovered was located in Regina, Saskatchewan, Canada—1,500 miles from my home in Columbus, Ohio. This was back in the '70s when there was a severe energy shortage when cars were backed up for blocks trying to get gas. The airlines were having the same problem. Before leaving New York, I went to a travel agent to buy a round-trip ticket to Regina. I was told, because of the shortage, I could only purchase a one-way ticket to Regina, and I got the only seat they had left. So, in total faith, I purchased the ticket and went back home to Columbus for Christmas break.

At home waiting for me was the enrolment package from Canadian Bible College. I quickly completed the package and sent it to the school. As Christmas break drew to a close, I still hadn't heard anything from the new school. I looked at the ticket I had already purchased wondering if I had done the right thing. Here it was the day before I was to leave for Regina, so I prayed, "Ok Lord, you told me to go, and I'm gonna go, but if I get stuck, it's up to you to get me unstuck!" Later that day, I received my one and only ever Western Union Telegram saying I had been accepted at Canadian Bible College for the coming semester!

The next day my cute girlfriend (later my wife Barb) drove me to the Pittsburgh, Pennsylvania, airport to fly to Regina. That was the closest airport I could fly out of because of the energy shortage. It was an unseasonably balmy 50 degrees for a day in January. Saying our tearful goodbyes, I boarded the plane still trusting the Lord.

The Regina airport back then had an old-fashioned design—the plane would land and stop on the runway, and then the passengers would disembark, walk across the runway and large open field to the mini-terminal. Shortly after crossing the northern U.S.-Canadian border, our plane landed; I stepped out of the plane and was stunned!

With the wind chill factor, it felt like it was 50 degrees BELOW ZERO! A 100-degree drop in temperature was a real shocker to my system! It was a very long distance to that terminal, and my parka was in my luggage; I was the only person running and yelling all the way to the terminal!

After I got my composure and folks around me stopped laughing, I dug out my parka and called a taxi. By the time the taxi came, it was dark outside. I shared my travel story with the taxi driver and the story of how I came to know Jesus. When we arrived at the school, she was crying a bit; I prayed with her and she only charged me half price. Now, there I was—standing in front of the small school. I walked in the front door and saw a light on my left coming from what seemed to be a micro bookstore. It was the day before the students were to arrive, all 200 of them, and an older lady was diligently organizing a pile of textbooks.

In my happy, cheerful voice, I loudly said, "Hi!" and the poor old gal nearly jumped over a chair! I, with long hair, a very large red beard, ragged hippie clothes, and sitting high on my shoulders tied to an aluminium frame was a giant brown canvas backpack—her reaction was understandable and in the instant, she probably thought she was seeing Big Foot.

I announced to her, "The Lord told me to come here, so now that I'm here, what do I do?" After she recovered, she said she was in the process of closing the bookstore but would call the Dean of Men first and tell him I was here. She did that, turned off the lights, locked the door, said, "Goodbye," and giving me a wide berth made a hasty exit.

I was left standing in the darkened building with just the dim security lights lit. Out of nowhere I heard the tapping of footsteps, and in the dim light about thirty feet away, a girl stopped and stared at me. With the lighting and shadows, she almost looked like a ghost! As we stared at each other, she asked, "Are you Nicky from Columbus, Ohio!" I was shocked! This living apparition knew my name!!

It turned out she had been on a mission trip to Thailand the summer before with my girlfriend and recognized me from her pictures! On top of that, she said that she worked in Admissions, and when she saw my late application come in, she connected my name from my girlfriend's conversations, and so put my application at the head of the pile. Now, I knew how I got accepted so quickly into the school. While we were talking, the Dean of Men showed up, and he took me over to the men's dorm.

On the way, he said he couldn't figure out how I got accepted because every bed in the dorm was filled. He said, "For now, I'll just put you in one of the guy's rooms for the night, and when the rest of the students show up tomorrow, we'll try to find a place for you off campus."

While walking down the hall between the dorm rooms, this skinny Canadian guy comes up to the Dean of Men and says, "Dean, my roommate just left and said he wouldn't be back for this semester." The Dean looked at me, looked at the skinny guy, then said to me, "Meet your new roommate!" Clearly, "The Voice" of God had spoken to me as He went before me and "made a way, where there seemed to be no way."

"And my God will supply all your needs according to His riches in glory in Christ Jesus."—Philippians 4:19 (NAS)

Postscript: One other little thing. When I arrived at the college, I had ZERO money to pay for the semester. Since the Lord told me to go and had worked out everything else for me to be there, I figured He would take care of the money as well. When administration asked me how I wanted to pay for the semester, I smiled and chuckled saying, "Good question; I have no clue!" When they learned I had done maintenance work in the past, they put me on a maintenance crew. I shoveled a lot of snow that winter and did other things around the college, and at the end of the semester, I walked away with nothing owed. PTL!!!

Oh, and by-the-way, my new roommate and I became lifelong friends and are in frequent contact to this day—46 years later.

The Wart and the Casket

Laying her 98-year-old Mother on the bed, she felt her go limp. No pulse. My most-favorite-Mother-in-law had passed from my sister-in-law's arms into the arms of Jesus. No drama—she passed peacefully into His presence—at home in the cozy apartment her son-in-law had built especially for her.

The first time I met my wife's very conservative parents, whose father was a pastor, was a bit of a jolt, not for me, but for them! I looked like, and actually was, a bit of a "hippie," with my long hair, torn jeans, flannel shirt, hiking boots, and a large bushy red beard. They must have thought their conservative daughter had gone off her rocker!

After we were married, and over the years, I fell deeply in love with my wife's parents and wonderful family. When guys at the lab would talk about how meddling and annoying their Mother-in-laws were, I'd brag about how great my Mother-in-law was! My wife's parents were special.

Dad told me one time about when he and Mother were doing missionary work back in the 1940s in the wild backwoods of Kentucky. It was a tough time for them because the main product in them hills was "Moonshine," bootleg whisky. The whisky boys were giving Dad a hard time because they were worried that if folks started giving their lives to Jesus, business would go down.

One day Dad drove up the dry old rocky riverbed, which was the only road back then, to preach at an evening service. After the service, a group of rough mountain men came out of the woods and surrounded dad and his car. Dad said he prayed for safety, didn't say a word to the men, got in his car, drove through the men back down the riverbed. Later he was told by one of the men that they were so angry and on edge, that if Dad would have said anything to them, they would have stoned him to death.

Mother often told me about those days when in the backwoods how whenever they ran out of food, or milk or diapers for the babies, that the Lord would bring those things to their doorstep. They didn't have much money, but she said the Lord always took care of them.

One evening while sitting in the kitchen, long after I'd married into the family, Mother told me about losing her sixteen-year-old son. He was an athlete who played football in high school. He had a paper route, and was well-loved by the community. One day he came home from school complaining about getting a stiff neck during typing class. A few days later he was gone.

Mother told me his death nearly tore her heart out. She grieved his loss; she grieved profoundly and for a long time. Holding her hand to her forehead, she tightly closed her eyes reliving the past and said to me, "It got so bad, that I was having trouble doing my duties at the church, and I really thought I was starting to lose my mind!" "Then one night during prayer when I felt I was at the end of myself with grief, Jesus seemed to come to me and touch my mind, and took my grief, and I knew everything would be ok. The next day I was fine and could function normally—Jesus really had taken my burden. I still missed my son, but everything was ok from then on."

Much later when Dad was in the hospital, Jesus again came to Mother and gave her a verse that made her realize that the Lord was going to take Dad home. The next day, he, too, passed into the arms of Jesus. And just a few days ago, unknown to my wife, the day before her Mother passed away, the Lord also gave her a special verse to bring comfort. Sitting in a restaurant for breakfast on the other side of the world in South East Asia, my wife who decided to read Ephesians during breakfast, was struck with the verse, "The Lord Himself is our peace." Throughout the day, she wondered why the Lord had so impressed this verse on her heart. Jesus had prepared her for her Mother's death just as Jesus had prepared her Mother for her dad's death. Both experienced peace straight from the heart of God.

Thinking back over the years, I recalled Mother being funny in her own way. She generally didn't get jokes, couldn't hold a tune, and in their younger years when Dad started teaching her how to drive, on her first lesson she backed straight up into a chicken coop, sending the chickens and feathers flying everywhere, and that was the end of her driving lessons! But she was awesome in a thousand other ways—in ways that count!

One time sitting at the large old farm table for dinner with my family and my in-laws that lived on a farm nearby I decided to tell a joke that was, well, a bit on the edge. I figured Mother wouldn't get it, so I told the joke and watched everyone having a good laugh and my brother-in-law was laughing so hard I'd never seen him turn that red! I was sitting there kind of proud of myself for launching a really funny joke past Mother, when I hear her from the head of the table calling my name. Mother said, "Can you explain that joke to me please?" Then it was my turn to turn red!!

Another time we were visiting Mother and had brought along our dog Sassy, a miniature Doberman. My family and I were sitting with

Mother at the table for lunch during one of our many Christmas vacation visits. Before eating, Mother would often remove her retainer from her mouth and put it in a napkin while she ate. This time after doing that, she unknowingly knocked it to the floor. One of my kids noticed and called my attention to it—just as we heard Sassy making some strange noises under the table.

When I looked under the table, I saw that Sassy had her paws tightly wrapped around the retainer licking off old yummy remains. Sassy looked up at me, and I recognized her look and realized Sassy was getting ready to turn Mother's retainer into a doggy chew! I dove under the table and retrieved the retainer—gave it back to Mother and before I could say anything about Sassy licking her retainer, she promptly popped it back into her mouth!

Mother was also a bit of word maven, and even in her nineties could, according to a tall and very smart friend of ours, "clean his clock," in the word game Boggle. That game along with Skip-bo and crossword puzzles kept her mind agile. But more important than the games in keeping her mind agile were all the missionaries and pastors she prayed for every day! She had a prayer manual that listed thousands of retired and current missionaries and pastors from around the world. It became so worn and full of notes, you could hardly read it! In 2006 we bought her a new one.

Now, 2012, as I thumb through that "new" one, it is also worn and tattered; I am simply amazed at the number of people she had prayed for including added notes of additional family members or special needs. Mother was in the full sense of the phrase, a "Prayer Warrior." And oh, how she prayed for all of her children and grandchildren, and great grandchildren—we will all miss her prayers profoundly!! And she knew her Bible well—during evening devotions on our visits she would often finish quoting by memory what we had started reading from the Bible.

By now, you're probably wondering what all this has to do with a wart and a casket. Well, Mother had expressed her wishes that she wanted an open-casket funeral. A couple years back she had developed a rather unbecoming wart on her nose. Now, near her death, it had become a very ugly witchy looking wart. Not that Mother cared much . . . at 98 she was past being concerned about looking fashionable.

On the day of her passing, in the morning during breakfast my sister-in-law was looking at her wart thinking how bad it looked. At lunchtime, she noticed the wart was gone! And three hours later, so was Mother! It was as if Jesus came down and performed His own special surgery to prepare her for her open-casket funeral. What a cool final gesture of love from our Lord Jesus to Mother.

Mother will be greatly missed; she will be a tough act to follow, and we will all greatly miss her prayers. But words cannot express the gratitude we have for the rich spiritual heritage she and Dad have left us. Mother is now happy in heaven to be with her Jesus who she has been looking forward to seeing since she was a young girl. And like my other brother-in-law said, "She will be rejoicing in heaven, but she will be walking—No driving, as Dad will see to that!"

"Precious in the sight of the Lord is the death of his saints." —Psalm 116:15

Postscript: Written in memory of my Most-Favorite-Mother-in-Law, what I always called her, who went to be with Jesus on January 9, 2012.

Answered Prayer Hanging on a Nail

I pulled on the wrench. It slipped off the nut. I sliced my knuckles against the engine block—blood drips down my black grease-covered fingers. Like usual, I yanked out my trusty-crusty handkerchief, wrapped it around my knuckles and kept working. I figured if I didn't cut myself, or stab myself with a screwdriver, or draw blood in some other way, then I wasn't doing a good job on my car! Just kidding, but I usually do get hurt while working on my cars. Anyway, I was in the process of changing the water pump on an old station wagon I had. It was a hand-me-down car from my parents so we could more easily haul our growing family around.

The day before, I backed out of my parking spot at a grocery store and noticed a little puddle of green antifreeze and thought to myself, "Whoa, I recognize that florescent green puddle! Poor guy, either his radiator has a leak, or his water pump is going bad." The next day I backed out of my parking spot at the library and saw another puddle of green antifreeze. Again, I thought to myself, "Poor fellow, except I think the poor fellow might be me!!" Getting out of the car, I popped open my hood and the wiring and motor block around my water pump were wet with antifreeze! "Yep, it be me!!" I said aloud.

Fortunately, the car hadn't started overheating yet, so I didn't have steam pouring out from under my hood with all the drama that comes along with an overheating engine. I drove to the auto store and purchased a replacement water pump and then drove to my grandfather's house and parked it in his large old two-car garage. Grandpa didn't mind me working on my car in his garage ... except for the time I tried to pull a motor out of my car and tied the pulley to a heavy pole laid across his garage roof trusses and they started to crack and could have brought his roof down. Other than that time, he was happy to have me there.

I'd changed lots of water pumps in the past and figured it would be a quick job. After draining the antifreeze and unclamping the hoses, I got a good view of the pump. I was able to wiggle the shaft so the bearings wearing out was probably the problem and explained the slow leak. However, the more I studied that water pump and how it was bolted to the block, I realized it was a configuration I'd never seen before. I consulted my handy car manual—whenever I got a car, I would buy an automotive manual for that make and year of car. The manual said that I needed to use a "special tool" to remove the water pump, or my timing chain would move and mess up the timing of my car! And I really didn't want that headache.

I called an auto parts store to find out how much this "special tool" would cost. They didn't carry the tool. I called another store, and they didn't carry it either. I called a more expensive auto parts store, but no luck there either. However, the parts counter guy said, "I know the tool you need, and it is critical to use on that model of car, and if you don't use it, it'll throw your timing off when you change your water pump. Your best bet is to call a dealer."

I call the dealer; they have the "special tool" but won't rent or loan it to me. The parts manager said, "I can try and special order it for you, but it will take several weeks to get. We even had a hard time getting one ourselves!" I couldn't afford to take my car to the dealer and be charged five times what it would cost me do to it myself.

Walking back out to my car in the garage, I prayed, "Lord, I need my car working . . . I have the water pump . . . I can't afford to have the dealer do it . . . and I don't have the 'special tool.' What do I do? In Jesus name, Amen." I looked up and saw a large old cast iron handle randomly hanging on a nail on the garage wall. **That** handle had been hanging on **that** nail since I was a little kid. I remember playing with the handle my dad had made for my grandfather when my dad worked in a grey iron foundry.

I picked up my car manual and looked at a picture of the "special tool". . . I looked at the handle on the nail and said out loud, "No way, Lord!!" I took the handle and stuck it down by the water pump. The two holes on the left side of the handle fit the two protruding studs and the arc of the handle went up and over the timing chain, and the single stud on the other side matched a hole on the right side of the handle. I bolted it into place, removed the old water pump, installed the new water pump, unbolted the handle, and finished bolting everything back into place.

I plopped myself down on the garage floor beside the car and pondered this amazing answer to prayer. The handle was exactly the right length. The holes were large enough to accommodate the stud diameter. The two holes on the left side of the handle were centered exactly the same distance apart as the side-by-side studs. The arc of the handle was just barely high enough to clear the timing chain. It was a heavy-duty cast-iron handle, so it could easily take the bolt pressure and not sag or bend. And on top of all that, the answer to my prayer—my "special tool" from God—had been hanging on that nail for almost twenty years!

". . . Your Father knows what you need even before you ask him." —Matthew 6:8 (NIV)

Black Friday & Little Faith

At 4:15 AM I hauled myself and my still-sleeping rear end out of bed all for the love of family. It was Black Friday, the day after Thanksgiving when stores have their sales to beat all sales! This was the first time I was going to join the infamous shopping-crazed mobs to save some money.

One daughter wanted a dash mounted GPS for her car for Christmas, and she and another daughter badly needed external hard drives to back up their dying laptops they'd been using for college. With no shave, no shower, not even a dab of deodorant, out the door I went. (I thought maybe the lack of deodorant would give me an edge getting through the crowds!) Driving down the road I said, "Lord, could you please save me a couple of hard drives for my daughters? They are such a good deal, and I know they're gonna sell fast . . . in Jesus name, Amen."

I arrive at Wal-Mart for the GPS at 4:45 AM and see people already going into the store! I was told it didn't open till 5 AM. The parking lot was packed, and I had to park way out on the edge. As I walked toward the store, I saw a bunch of other folks running towards the entrance clearly on a mission to buy—-I resisted the urge to run!

Once inside, it was like the parking lot outside! I headed for a cart, but they were all gone! The aisles were nearly gridlocked with people and carts; some carts were piled nearly five-feet high with bargains. Numerous police with darting eyes and wearing frowns were positioned around the store for mob control since someone died in a Wal-Mart stampede last year. I politely pushed . . . apologized, bumped . . . apologized, slid carts sideways . . . apologized, and physically worked my way to the electronics department at the back of the store.

Reaching the counter, I started waving to get the frenzied clerk's attention. I asked her where the cheap GPSes were located. As the clerk opened her mouth to answer me, a very tall sizable lady moved in right beside me and asked her the same question. Answering her instead, the clerk pointed her to way over to somewhere I couldn't see. The tall lady turned and made a beeline in that direction, so I jumped in formation right behind her. She was not so polite! She pushed her way through the crowd, and after a few minutes of following in her people-wake, she stopped, leaned forward, moved to my right, and there they were! A pile of bright green GPS boxes. In my heart I said, "Wow, thanks Lord for the tall lady!" I grabbed a box and made my way to a check out at the front of the store.

Happy to be out of there with life and limb still intact, my next stop was Radio Shack for the two hard drives on sale, which was located next to the Wal-Mart. Again, I saw folks rushing into the store, and again I resisted the urge to run! Radio Shack is a small store but was stuffed with customers who were huddled around sale items like vultures around roadkill. The hard drive they had on sale was nearly half its normal price and was made by one of the top three hard drive makers. I asked the attendant if he still had two hard drives left. He looked at me like, "You've got to be kidding me." He said they were some of the first items that sold out when their doors opened hours ago.

I asked if he could check and see if another Radio Shack near where I lived had any left. This time he gave me a, "you're-wasting-my-time look," but obviously out of duty, checked any way. Nope, they were gone, too, from that store, and again, were the first things to sell out. That was a bummer because of all the store ads I checked, Radio Shack had by far the best price on the hard drive. I thought to myself, "Well, the Micro Center computer store was only a few miles down the road, and they had the next best price." I got there at 6:20 AM and a line was forming at the door. Thinking they were going to open at 6:30, I get in line only to find out they wouldn't open their doors till 8 AM!

Hungry and not feeling like standing that long in line, I headed for the McDonald's across the street where I ate breakfast and watched the news on a large screen TV. At 7:40, on the way back across the street to the Micro Center, I suddenly remembered there was another Radio Shack halfway up the strip mall from the Micro Center. Deciding to kill some more time, I thought I would go in and see what other things Radio Shack had on sale.

Not surprisingly, the store was crowded, and I milled around for a while looking at sale stuff. Eventually, an attendant asked me if I needed any help? I started to shake my head "No" but ended up saying, "Do you by chance have two of the hard drives left that are on sale?" He said, "Yes! We only have two left; would you like them?!"

My mouth dropped open and almost hit the floor, and it was as if the Lord said to me, "See, I saved you two hard drives, just like you asked." Then down in my heart, I felt something like a wink and a smile from the Lord saying, "Oh ye of little faith!!"

—Matthew 8:26 (KJV)

Postscript: When I first published this story on my FaithStoriesOnline blog, my youngest daughter Brittany left the following comment...

"Wow. Poppy. That was an amazing story! And an encouraging story, it brought me to a few tears...especially towards the end when God said to you, 'Oh ye of little faith.' God is so good, and He really does give us what we need or even simply what we want as a blessing. And now—Heather and I know what we're getting for Christmas! Wahoo!"

Poop-Brown and the Protection of God

Little could I have imagined how important my old ugly Jeep would become to my cousin and me. There are times where God answers your prayer, and though it's not exactly what you prayed for, because He knows the future, it's always what's best!

A month before getting married, I needed a van to drive my new bride and our wedding gifts up to Saskatchewan, Canada, to continue my education at Canadian Bible College. I very specifically prayed, "Lord, if possible, I would like to have a Ford van within my price range, with windows all around it so I can see better when driving the thing, with inside access to the engine for the cold winters up there, and with a stick shift transmission. Amen!" A week later, my dad called me and said he saw a van for sale a couple of streets over. That day I looked at it, and it was everything I'd asked for to a tee!! What a wedding present from the Lord!

A decade or so later I found myself needing another car. We'd just purchased an old farmhouse for a home, so there was very little money left for a car. Recalling my previous van prayer, I boldly prayed, "Lord! I need a cheap, reliable car . . . and I'd really like a Jeep!" In my mind,

I was optimistically seeing a "cool" bright cherry red manly outdoorsman-climbing-the-high-rugged-mountain-roads-four-wheel-drive kind of Jeep.

Well, God did answer my prayer, and I did get a cheap Jeep, but it wasn't exactly the "cool" bright cherry red manly-outdoorsman-climbing-the-high-rugged-mountain-roads-four-wheel-drive kind of Jeep that I had envisioned.

It was more like the "NOT cool" box-shaped U.S. Postal Service kind of Jeep! After it had served its purposes for the postal service, in order to sell them, they painted their well-used fleet brown, a sort of poop-brown, to cover up the postal service logos. It also came with large side mirrors like elephant ears, a steering wheel that was on the right where most American passengers sit, and it came complete with only ONE seat . . . and NO reverse! So, you always had to pay attention to how you parked since you could only go in one direction . . . forward.

Actually, it was such an oddity that it was fun to drive, but I must say that steering on the right side like postal carriers took some getting use to, especially going around corners where you felt like you were dragging your butt on the curb!

Now, part one of God's protection for me:

One late afternoon on a snowy winter day, I was sitting stuck in traffic at the end of an entrance ramp leading onto the freeway where they were doing some road work. This made it difficult to get into the flow of speeding traffic in the left two lanes. I was sitting there happily humming to myself since the Jeep also didn't have a radio.

While waiting, an odd noise behind me quickly crept into my consciousness. Looking in my big side mirror on the left, I saw a large, white Cadillac start into a spin on the slick icy freeway. Everything seemed to slow as I watched it circle once, then twice, and without hitting any other car, slam into my left side, lifting my Jeep up in the air to nearly a 45-degree angle. The Cadillac bounced off my Jeep, and as my Jeep slammed back to earth, the Cadillac crashed into the guardrail on the other side of the freeway!

All the traffic had stopped; I jumped out and ran to the Cadillac where a shaking middle-aged woman emerged crying and shouting at me, "Are you OK; ARE YOU OK!!??" I assured her I was just fine and explained that my seat was on the right side of my Jeep—opposite the side of impact. In my heart I prayed, "Thank you, Jesus, for giving me a Jeep with a seat on the "wrong" side! Had I been sitting where most people sit, I probably would have been very seriously injured!"

Part two, God's protection for my cousin:

That crazy old Jeep was still drivable after the hit, so I drove it for the next couple of years and then gave it to my cousin who needed a car. On April 1st, I get a call from my cousin apologizing for totaling the Jeep in a car crash! I said, "Yeah, yeah. April Fools!!" He said, "Seriously, I totaled the Jeep!!" "Yeah, yeah," I said. Then his dad, my uncle, gets on the phone. "It's true Nicky! I'm standing here next to it in a junkyard, and IT IS TOTALED!!" Finally, I believed my uncle.

My cousin explained that he had been going about 50 miles-an-hour on a busy, two-way highway. Not far ahead, a guy suddenly pulls out into my cousin's lane to go around someone. He can't get back in his lane. The right side of the road had a deep ravine with telephone poles and no room for my cousin to pull off without flipping the Jeep and smashing into a pole. The left oncoming lane was packed with traffic, so he couldn't go there. In that instant my cousin slams on his brakes, and this guy smashes right into the front of the Jeep at full speed! . . . a head-on collision that might have been, "The End!" for my cousin except for how the Jeep was built.

The old Jeep's body sat much higher off the ground than a normal car, so the damaging force of the impact went underneath my cousin. The man in the other car was hurt so badly that they had to fly him out by helicopter to a nearby hospital. And my cousin? He only got a split lip from hitting the steering wheel. Another huge "Praise the Lord!"

God may not always give us what we ask for, but as our all-knowing, loving Heavenly Father, He will for sure—always give us what we need. Even if that means a poop-brown Jeep!

"...how much more will your Father who is in heaven give good things to those who ask Him!" —Matthew 7:11 (NKJV)

A Prayer and a Puke

After parking at the Canadian border office north of Fargo, North Dakota, my new bride of one week and I started digging out our driver's licenses to show the border guard. When my new bride turned her head and looked deeply into my eyes and sweetly said, "My purse! My PURSE!! My purse has my driver's license, and I must have left it in Wheeling, West Virginia, at my parent's house!!" So much for sweet words! Now we were in a panic! In all the rush to leave on our honeymoon and drive West, she had forgotten her purse.

My classes started the next day at Canadian Bible College in Regina, Saskatchewan, Canada. In those days there was no overnight delivery of anything, so it would take days to get her ID. We were stuck, so I prayed, "Lord I'll have to leave my new bride here while I drive on to school—Just kidding Lord! Seriously Lord, we need to get across the border, both of us. Please help us, in Jesus name." The moment I quit praying, I felt like I was supposed to take our wedding album into the office with us.

It was not a busy border crossing and on entering the office, we only saw two officers. I got out my driver's license, laid down our wedding album on the counter, and fearfully told the officer we needed to cross the border but we had a problem—my new wife had forgotten her ID. The other officer asked about the pictures. The next thing I know we're all standing there looking at the album—I'm telling them wedding stories; they're laughing, and the four of us are having a great old time! When we finished with the pictures, they said we could go on across the border and wished us well with our new married life. Praise you, Jesus!!

Before leaving school the year before I had made arrangements to rent a cute little basement apartment for the coming school year. I even had the landlady's approval to bring a small pet since I'm a critter person. On arriving at the apartment, I introduced my new bride to the landlady and my furry little wedding present—an eleven-inch white, albino ferret. She thought the ferret, named Goofus, looked adorable! Much to our surprise and dismay, at the end of our first month in our cute little basement apartment, the landlady threw us out! I felt really bad that this might give the school a bad name so went to talk to the Dean of Married Students and told him what happened.

The next day he called me in his office and said, "I know about your little pet, but she said it was six feet long! She was afraid it might climb into her bedroom and eat her alive in the middle of the night! We've had students renting from her for years and in general she sounded much different than she had in the past, so, don't worry about it; I think she might be going through menopause." Whew! Another Praise the Lord!

We were told it was going to be very difficult to find another apartment with all the local colleges already in session. Still, we prayed and with a lead from another married couple at the college, right off the bat found another basement apartment at the same price and twice the size! The downside was it didn't have any hot water, and the wall closets were so cold from the extended subzero weather, we kept our frozen meat and ice cream in with our jackets and boots. But the upside was it was another answer to prayer and turned into a great basement apartment that was large enough to entertain friends. We were very thankful and praised the Lord!

Before we got kicked out of our first apartment, my new bride started looking for a job. This was crucial because we only had enough money for one month of school and rent. She had graduated that spring with her bachelor's degree, so we thought that would be helpful in her finding a job. She interviewed for a job as a stenographer at the office of the Royal Canadian Mounted Police. That's when we discovered she needed a work permit. However, we were informed by the Canadian Immigration Office that in order to get a work permit, she would have to show that she had a job promised to her and that it was a job no other Canadian wanted! What a hurdle; it looked like a total impossibility!

We brought this up as a prayer request at a church we had started attending. Soon after a lady contacted my wife and said she had a position she was having trouble keeping filled. She was the Director of Housekeeping at the Regina Inn and needed a housing keeping maid. The Regina Inn was the premiere hotel in Saskatchewan and had very high standards, which explained the high turnover of maids. My poor new bride was going from proudly receiving her college degree to cleaning toilets!

The Director of Housekeeping filled out the document we needed, and we took it to the immigration officer. He was a big, burly rather loud gentleman who said he was in a rush for a lunch meeting but would look at our paperwork. He sat down, glanced through it, signed it, told us to give it to his assistant, and left. Next door in the assistant's office, I handed her the signed paper; she glanced at it and got this weird look on her face. She said, "I don't know why he signed this giving you permission to work because this now makes him over quota!" Nevertheless, she processed the papers and gave my new bride her work permit!! Our hearts sang with praise, "Thank you, dear Jesus, for this permit we shouldn't have!"

My new bride came home exhausted from her first day on the job. It was a humbling experience, and though she was grateful for the job, started praying, "Lord, would it at all be possible to find a better job?" The second day on the job, she was cleaning a toilet and suddenly puked in the toilet! The Director of Housekeeping found out about her throwing up in the toilet and asked if she had any other skills, to which my new bride answered that she had been a switchboard operator in college. The Housekeeping Director made a call, and it turned out there was an opening for a switchboard operator at the front desk! Incredibly, another Praise the Lord!!!

During my time in college that year, my new bride happily worked the switchboard. A few months later, she even got to be part of the staff welcoming the Prime Minister of Canada to the Regina Inn, and at another time, to meet George Beverly Shea, the key soloist for the Billy Graham Crusades.

By faith—we moved from a prayer . . . to a puke . . . to God's plan. Praise the Lord!

"I will praise you, O Lord my God, with all my heart; I will glorify your name forever." —Psalm 86:12 (NIV)

~~ The End ~~

Photo Attribution:

Cover photo by Gerd Altmann: https://pixabay.com/users/geralt-9301/.

Chapter photos provided by: https://pixabay.com/.

Pixabay License:

Free for commercial use

No attribution required

—Bonus Stories—

<<>>

38

Sold Our Home on the R-A-D-I-O

<<>>

With my first real job after graduating from college, my wife and I purchased an old farmhouse in a low-income neighborhood—a great buy, or so I thought at the time. I figured it would go up in value...it never did. It was an original homestead in the area and was over a hundred years old with two floors and a huge attic that made it three stories tall. It had a very large yard with a century-worn old red barn in the back.

The first house on the street corner beside our driveway was painted a bright fluorescent green—so bright, in fact, it almost hurt your eyes to look at it. New to the neighborhood, I wanted to find out what kind of "nut" would paint their house that color. It seemed capable of glowing in the dark!

The sound of the doorbell brought my new neighbor into view. He was a tall and very elderly dignified looking gentleman with a cane and was wearing large dark sunglasses. Introducing himself as Ernest, he invited me in and in short order was telling me all kinds of stories about the area, especially about the great flood that hit Columbus, Ohio, way back in the year "nineteen-O-and-six." Later I learned the flood was actually in 1913, but at his age, being seven years off didn't mean much. Anyway, we quickly became friends. Then the question.

"Hey, Ernest, why is your house painted such a bright green color?"

"Wel-l-l," he drawled, "I'm legally blind, but I can still see some. As my eyes got worse, I started having trouble finding my house when I got off the bus. Then I got the green idea, and I haven't had a problem finding it since!" he said with a grin.

Soon after, I discovered that Ernest loved Jesus like myself, and during the five years we lived there; we had some good talks about the Lord. In fact, Ernest had such a passionate desire that others come to know his Savior too that he gave my three toddlers each a little green Gideon New Testament—he certainly had a thing about green!

His bright green garage bordered our driveway with just a few inches between the two; our drive went up a little hill, which put the drive on a diagonal about three feet high from the bottom of Ernest's garage. One day while working out in the backyard, I heard a loud "BOOM!" with a crunching metal sound following. Running around to the source of the sound, I saw this big old bronze-colored Buick half in our driveway, and half stuck into the side of Ernest's empty garage. The front end was suspended in midair, filling the emptiness of his garage. Bright green concrete blocks were laying everywhere.

Running over, I yanked open the door and shouted over the motor, "Are you okay??"

Reaching across the elderly woman, I turned off her car's engine.

With her voice quivering she said, "Yes, I'm fine—just a little rattled; I have a cast on my right foot, and when I went to hit the brake, my foot slipped off and hit the gas, and I guess my cast got stuck under the brake pedal!" And that's when she shot up our little driveway hill and through the side of Ernest's garage.

The squad came, checked her out and took her home. By this time, Ernest was standing by me beside his garage. Knowing he couldn't see, I said, "Hey, Ernest, you got a big ole hole in the side of your garage!"

Smiling, he said, "One of the good things about being blind is—the garage looks fine to me!"

When we bought the old farmhouse, we bought it on a land contract that ballooned in five years. That meant in five years we would have to pay the old German man who we bought the house from the balance we owed on it. Being young, that seemed far, far away; I had no idea how quickly time would pass and land us in a financial mess.

During those five years, sadly the cool old man passed away, and the house went to his wife. Soon after, she, too, passed away, and the house went to their two daughters. One was nice; one was nasty. There was such a fuss between the two sisters about our mortgage payment that we had to send two checks with half the amount to each sister separately—neither sister trusted the other to handle the money as a single account.

Reaching the end of our land contract after five years, the two sisters understandably wanted their money for the farmhouse. For many months prior, we had been trying to sell the house; however, there were two major strikes against the property. First, it was "atypical" of the area because nobody else had a barn, so the FHA (Federal Housing Administration) would not approve a loan on the house.

And second, it was considered a fixer-upper...being over a hundred years old; it still needed a lot of work. We even brought back the original realtor who sold it to us to help us try to sell the place again. Those that were in the market for buying a house didn't want a fixer-upper that old, and those that were looking for affordable housing couldn't get an FHA loan because it was atypical.

We were stuck, and things looked mighty grim!

On Wednesday before the last week when the balance on the farmhouse was due, the nasty sister called and said, "If you don't get me my money by next week Friday at noon, I will sue you for all you've got!!" That's when I got out my big old rickety wooden ladder, climbed to the top of our three-story roof, laid hands on the house and prayed that the Lord would make-a-way for us to be able to sell our old farmhouse.

Saturday morning before that final painful week, my wife and I prayed, "Lord, we certainly don't want to be sued, but we don't know what to do. We need Your help!"

Sitting on the bed watching our twin daughters play with their baby brother in our large farmhouse bedroom on that summer Saturday afternoon, my wife had the radio tuned to a Christian station. A program called, "Trade-E-Ola," was airing at the time. Folks would sell or trade things like used vacuum cleaners, cookware, toys, bicycles, etc. My wife suddenly looks up at me as I walk into the room and says, "I wonder if they would accept a house for sale on Trade-E-Ola?"

She calls the show. "Lady, we've never sold a house over the radio before, but we'll give it a try!"

We prayed and waited, listening for my wife's recorded message about the house. She had called near the end of the show, so we weren't sure if it'd even make it on the air or not, but we prayed it would since the show broadcast only on Saturdays. As we saw it, this was our last hope. Then, like music to our ears, we heard her recorded message loud and clear on the good ole R-A-D-I-O! In reality, it seemed pretty crazy to us that we were resorting to trying to sell a house on an old pots and pans radio show, but we certainly were!

The weekend passed, and the clock started ticking down to Friday when the money was due in full.

On Monday a lady called; she was looking for a house with some storage area for her son's drywall business and had heard my wife's message on Trade-E-Ola about the house with a barn on the property.

Tuesday, nothing.

Wednesday morning the nasty sister calls again with a vivid reminder, "If you don't have my money or a buyer by 12 o'clock noon Friday, then you can plan on seeing me in court!!"

On Wednesday afternoon, the lady that called on Monday calls again and wants to look at the property. That evening she comes over.

Soon after opening up the conversation about the house, my wife finds herself saying to this complete stranger, "I believe in 'zaps' from the Lord, and we are trusting Him about the sale of the farmhouse." To my wife's complete surprise, the lady echoed, "I believe in 'zaps' from the Lord, too."

A nice chat continued briefly about the Lord and their families. Then, my wife explained the difficulty of getting a loan on the house, to which the lady replied, "I don't think that'll be a problem; when my husband died, he left me a large tract of land (in a wealthy section of town we found out later). I can use that for collateral with the bank if I decide to buy." (In actuality, her "collateral" was such that buying our property was like her buying a loaf of bread!)

Thursday, nothing. Friday's coming.

Friday arrives. This is it. We feel like it's our D-Day or rather Dread Day in our "Oh ye of little faith" moment. We didn't know what this Friday would bring. We had prayed and had done what we could. I was at work and continued to pray while waiting and doing my job.

At home, my wife went about her morning duties with our three small children...8 o'clock....9....10 o'clock. The clock seems to be in slow motion racing towards 12-noon, our deadline when the nasty sister was going to pounce on us. My wife remembers the deafening silence of that morning well.

Then, at 11 AM the silence was broken by the sound of the ringing phone. With anxiety and excitement, my wife says, "Hello" and doesn't remember much else except the words, "I'll buy your house." ZAP! God rescues us!

We call the nasty sister and tell her we have a buyer.

We give loud praises and thanks to the God of the Bible who heard our cry for deliverance, chuckling a bit that He could even use a Trade-E-Ola R-A-D-I-O show!

There was no mistaking it; LITERALLY, at the 11th hour, the Lord rescued us!

We would have preferred more of a time buffer, but it seems like it was our turn to experience the old saying, "God is rarely early, but never late."

And so it was.

<<>>

"Wait for the LORD; be strong and take heart and wait for the LORD."
—-Psalms 27:14 (NIV)

<<>>

Postscript: I recently found a similar quote and thought it was worth sharing. "God is never late and rarely early. He is always exactly right on time—His time." —Dillon Burroughs

<<>>

The previous bonus story was taken from the book below.

To see the book below and Nick's other books go to: AuthorNick.com[1]

<<>>

---

1. https://authornick.com/

YOU CAN'T
GO WRONG
TRUSTING
GOD
A Collection of
True Stories
NICK NICHOLS

Not by Sight

<<>>

Sitting there at her sewing machine, my wife gave me her attention as I came into the room saying, "Well, I've got our road trip mapped out; it should only take three months, through three countries, and around 15,000 miles." She stopped sewing, looked at me with her loving, caring eyes, and sweetly said loudly, "Are you crazy! You can't be serious, we have three little children!" But I WAS serious.

In 1987 my wife had quit her teaching job at a business university to stay home with our young children; I had quit my job as an environmental scientist with a state agency to strike out on my own as an environmental consultant, so for the time being, we were both jobless. Now, with time on my hands, I wanted to come up to speed on some current environmental issues, so my plan was to fly to an environmental conference in Tennessee and then fly to Washington,

D.C. to discuss some energy ideas with a friend who had helped design the COMSAT satellite system, and then fly home.

Another travel plan developed, however, when my wife said, "I'm not working, and you're not working, so why don't we drive the trip and turn it into a family vacation." So, sitting down with a map, I looked at driving from Columbus, Ohio, to Knoxville, Tennessee for the conference, and then realized we weren't far from Macon, Georgia, where I had some relatives, and that wasn't far from Sarasota, Florida, where some of our good friends lived, and that wasn't far from West Palm Beach on the other side of Florida where my wife had some relatives, and traveling up the East Coast, we had more friends and relatives right up to Boston.

And since I was on a roll at that point, the plan just kept rolling along from Boston to Chicago, down to Little Rock, Arkansas, to the bottom of Texas, down to Mexico City continuing to Guatemala City, up the West coast of Mexico, into Arizona, California, Oregon, Washington, up into British Columbia and across Canada, back into the States through Minnesota, Wisconsin, Illinois, Indiana, and finally........back to Columbus, Ohio!

That's why . . . when I presented my travel plans to my wife and at this point she clearly saw that she got a whole lot more than what she had originally bargained for, and so reacted with, "Are you crazy?" One good friend with great concern said, "Nick, I think you've gone off the deep end this time." My reaction was to go buy a twenty-year-old VW camper van!!

In the following weeks, we packed up the van with supplies for us and the kids and lots of spare parts and plenty of oil for the van. My son wasn't potty trained yet, so we had white disposable diapers stuck everywhere! Before leaving, a friend of ours gave us a little 3x3-inch plaque with a Scripture verse on it that read, "We walk by faith, not by sight." (2 Corinthians 5:7) We set the little plaque in a prominent place on our dashboard as it seemed the perfect motto for our trip.

The next day my wife, our five-year-old twin daughters, and two-year-old son climbed in the old van as I pulled the sliding side door shut. It was like boarding Noah's Ark only without the critters and the rain. Pulling left out of our middle-class suburban driveway, we worked our way to the interstate, and we were off!

I was enjoying the drive south out of flat Columbus, Ohio, the kids were playing in the back of the roomy camper van, my wife was sitting in the passenger seat reading her Bible and watching the rolling hills grow larger and greener with trees as we drove further south. The sky was a beautiful blue with wispy clouds, and all was serene as the old van purred along.

After passing through Kentucky into Tennessee, I noticed a lack of power as the van attempted to climb the hills. I chalked it up, however, to the van being a four cylinder that was loaded with family and supplies. But as we drove along, and as the hills got steeper, I became more concerned about the steady decline in engine power; then about half way up a very long high hill, it happened.

I felt the van jerk, and looking out the rear-view mirror, I saw a huge cloud of gray smoke coming out of the back of the van where the engine was located. I had flashbacks of a burning van I was in earlier in my life that caused me to have visions of flames and a possible explosion. I yelled to my wife to get in the back of the van with the kids and instructed her that when I slowed down, I wanted her and the kids to jump out the sliding side door. My intent was to get the van away from them in case it burst into flames or exploded.

In preparation for the exit, my wife pulled open the side door; then slowing way down, I yelled back to them, "JUMP!" Instantly, they all bailed out holding hands, tumbling into the tall grass by the road while I kept going till they were a safe distance away; then, I pulled the van to the side of the road, turned off the engine, yanked on the emergency brake, jumped out and ran back through the cloud of smoke to my family. We stood there and watched, but surprisingly, the big gray cloud drifted away, and nothing more seemed to be happening. Still, we waited.

After a good while, I walked back to the van, put my hand against the engine lid to see if something might still be smoldering on the inside, but the lid felt reasonably cool. Lifting the lid with great caution to inspect the engine, I feared that I might see all the wiring and parts burnt to a crisp like in my previous van, but to my complete surprise, they all looked fine, only covered with a layer of oil!

Checking the oil in the engine, there was not a drop on the dipstick, but since I had purchased plenty of oil before leaving Ohio, I was in good shape. After refilling the engine with oil, I cautiously tried to start the motor. To my surprise, it started! However, it was running very rough, like it was only running on three cylinders instead of four, and the smoke started blowing out of the exhaust pipe again. Going to the back of the van and putting my hand into the exhaust cloud, I felt it was oily smoke and not a fire-based smoke. Obviously, something had happened to one or more of the pistons, and oil was being blown out of the engine.

The van seemed drivable, so we all got back in, and slowly, very slowly, we continued climbing the long, high hill. Soon, we came to a filling station; we needed gas, and I needed to check the oil. While my wife and kids made a potty run, I started filling the tank with gas and noticed a small puddle of oil forming under the van and realized the engine problem was even more serious than I had originally thought. Praying, I said, "Lord, what do we do now? Is this the end of the trip? We really need your help! Thank you ... in the name of Jesus." As soon as I finished praying, my eyes were drawn to a white plastic audio cassette lying in the dirt in a nearby parking spot.

Letting go of the gas pump handle, I walked over and picked up the cassette. The side I picked up was blank, but when I turned it over, I saw that it was a music cassette by a Christian band I recognized. It was Petra's album, *Not of This World*, and again my eyes were drawn to the middle song called—"Not by Sight." I thought about the plaque from our friend that was sitting on our dashboard and was reminded that indeed we are to walk not by sight, but by faith! Right then and there, I decided that no matter how bad our situation "looked," we would go on in faith trusting the Lord.

Filling the van up with oil and with a full tank of gas, we headed back out to the road and continued coasting down hills, and climbing them at a snail's pace, all the time fogging the folks behind us with oil smoke. After about ten miles and a couple of stops to dump more oil in the van, the engine seemed to be getting more critical. It was starting to get dark as evening closed in, and I began to wonder what to do. In another mile or so, we saw a truck weigh station, and I decided to pull in. There were only a couple of guys working in the isolated station with no trucks around that needed weighing.

After going into the little building to inquire about a nearby auto repair shop, one of the guys said he had a friend that worked on VWs but more as a hobby rather than as a business, but he thought he might be able to help. He assured me that there were no auto repair shops nearby, and his friend was my best bet for getting the engine repaired. He called his mechanic friend, who suggested that we stay the night at a nearby state park, and then drive, if I could, to his place in the morning. He said he lived back in the woods, and we would never find his place in the dark. He gave us directions to the park and his place and planned on seeing me the next day at 9 a.m.

We limped our way to the park, paid for a camping site, parked the van and got ready for bed by setting up the beds in the van, but before drifting off to sleep, we prayed and thanked the Lord for a safe place to stay and for a plan to get the van fixed. Waking early the next morning and figuring this was probably going to take more than one day to fix, I got out the only "tent" we had which was a screen house, set it up, and moved the family, sleeping bags, food, water, and cooking stuff into the screen house.

My family looked like they were in a cage for all to see as folks walking by on the nearby trail looked rather strangely at them. In my wife's own words, she recounts, "I remember feeling very silly; everybody knows you use a tent with sides to go camping, not a see-through screen house! What kind of novice campers were we?? Obviously, we hadn't taken Camping 101 or if we took it, we must have royally failed it!!! The passers-by had no idea we had a camper van that was in the shop being repaired."

This was back before the days of affordable cell phones, so as I drove off, there was no way for me to stay in contact with my wife or to let the mechanic know I was coming. Leaving early to make sure I had plenty of time to get to the mechanic's house, I followed his map through the narrow, secluded wooded park roads. It seemed like I was about half way there when the van died—it just quit. It was 8 a.m.; I got out my tools and tried working on the engine, cleaning oil off the connections and such to try to get it started again. By 9 a.m. I was hot and thirsty and realized I had left all the water with my family, and there was no other water in sight.

Hunting around in the van, I found a quart of apple sauce; figuring that it had liquid in it, I drank the whole jar which did little to quench my thirst. Back out on the engine, I needed to get it started to get to the mechanic. About twenty minutes later, I stood up from the engine and felt something funny happening inside of me! All of a sudden, I felt as if I had just drank a very large glass of cool water!! I thought, "Wow!" It took about twenty minutes for my body to break down the fiber in the apple sauce to liquid, and I felt completely refreshed and no longer thirsty! Loudly I said, "Thank you, Jesus!!"

A few minutes after that, I saw a large tractor coming toward me—it was the mechanic! He said he figured I may have broken down on the way, so he came looking for me. He hooked up my van, towed it to his house, and drug it up a very steep hill to his large garage. Even in perfect running order, my van never would have made it up his hill. In short order, he found the problem—a hole had been blown through a piston head! That explained the loss of power and the large gray oil cloud that traveled with us.

Our answer-to-prayer-mechanic said it would take him a few days to get parts and rebuild the engine, so we'd needed to stay at the park till he was finished. He drove me back to the park where we lived in our screen house for all to see for three days. I got pretty good at changing my clothes in a sleeping bag though my wife and family chose to take the long walk to the shower house. We literally came to understand what it meant to "live in a glass house." More than a cliché, it became our awkward reality.

After the van was fixed, our friendly and extremely helpful Tennessee mechanic picked me up and took me back to his place, and I drove our new happy, healthy, purring-like-a-kitten van back to my family.

It was the start of a new day and the beginning of our three-month, three-country, three-kid, 15,100-mile trip. We loaded up the van, piled in, pulled the ark door shut, and we were off . . . with a new engine and a renewed faith.

<<>>

"For we walk by faith, not by sight." —2 Corinthians 5:7 (KJV)

<<>>

Postscript: Our trip covered all the places mentioned except we never made it to Guatemala because we were robbed on a subway train underneath Mexico City and banditos got my passport—but that's a story detailed in a later chapter.

[This story is dedicated to Karen and Denise DM. who met up with us in Boston during our long road trip. Karen also took the photo of our family aboard the USS Constitution at the top of the story. Thank you Karen and DD, you guys are awesome! —Nick]

<<>>

The previous bonus story was taken from the book below.

To see the book below and Nick's other books go to: AuthorNick.com[1]

<<>>

"For we walk by faith, not by sight." —2 Corinthians 5:7 (KJV)

---

1. https://authornick.com/

Walking by
FAITH
not by
SIGHT
A Collection of True Stories
NICK NICHOLS

3 Angels 3 Encounters 3 Blessings

<<>>

The following three encounters by the following three men will never and can never be forgotten by them . . .

ANGEL #1

Late at night, five blocks down the street, my great Uncle Paul realized he was in a heap of trouble!! Earlier in the morning, he had taken a taxi to the large, downtown convention center that was about ten blocks away. After the sessions and then a late-night dinner with another salesman, Uncle Paul had decided to walk off his dinner and think about the events of the day by walking back to his hotel instead of taking a cab.

When he was about halfway back, around block number five, he found creeping into his consciousness an awareness of being surrounded by gang graffiti taking on odd hues in the light of the street lamps. Gangs of young men sat together on the steps of some of the dilapidated tenant buildings and appeared to be just lookin' for trouble. Uncle Paul focused as best he could and kept walking, passing more gangs and trying not to make eye contact. Only three blocks to go. Now, a gang trailing behind him started yelling, "Hey old man! I need some money! Got any extra cash on you?" Laughter followed with increasingly ramped up jeering and taunting.

No police in sight, nowhere to run, heart pounding out of his chest, he wondered how a grown man could make such a stupid mistake to walk alone so late at night in a shady part of the city, but it was far too late to think about that now. Years before, he had seared into his kids' minds, "Never, ever walk alone at night; always stay in a group, especially in a big city," but here he was—not following his own wisdom. Being a victim of a mugging was imminent.

While bracing himself for the first blow, a colossal powerfully built man matches my uncle's stride and instead of landing a vicious attack, takes his arm and with some authority in his voice says, "Keep looking straight ahead and keep walking." The gang dropped back as if on cue, and his newly arrived personal escort walked him the last three blocks to the steps of his hotel, giving my uncle a little friendly push to start him up the steps. Uncle Paul turned to thank the man, but in that blink of an eye, there was no one to thank. His companion was gone! With a puzzled face, he looked up at the doorman at the top of the steps who had seen my uncle and his new friend. But with raised eyebrows, he looked just as puzzled and shrugged his shoulders while opening the door for another guest.

Years later when my uncle recounted this incident to me, I'll never forget the confidence in his voice and the look in his eye when he reflected, "The Lord sent an angel that night to protect me! I don't care if anyone believes me or not. I was there, and I know that I know that I know what I experienced." Then, as a side note while chuckling a bit half to himself and half to me, "With all the brawn and adrenaline pumping through the veins of those teenage gang members, God certainly knew what he was doing by sending a powerhouse angel dude as a body guard—an escort that was no match for those rough, tough smart-aleck kids—one escort not to be messed with!"

That walk back to my uncle's hotel produced an encounter never to be forgotten, remaining vivid in Uncle Paul to the end of his life.....and I've often wondered which angel came to escort Uncle Paul through those Pearly Gates . . . H-m-m....maybe, just maybe . . .

ANGEL #2

Back in the late1980s, a friend and I decided to attend an inventors' meeting where a Congressman would be speaking about new legislation promoting future innovation. It was held on a Thursday night at our local Center of Science and Industry, locally known as COSI, located in the heart of our downtown city.

My friend and I worked together in a laboratory, and I had recently finished a simple innovation that would (and did) save our laboratory tens of thousands of dollars over the following years and only cost $300 for me to build. My chemist friend, who was from Russia, held ten international patents. Recently, we had been kicking around another invention idea in the lab, so we were serious attendees.

After the informative session, we gathered for drinks and hors d'oeuvres with other inventors, venture capital guys looking for investments and some inventor hopefuls, including myself, for some chat time. Standing there with a cocktail sandwich in my hand waiting to talk to a venture capital guy, I was thinking about the fact that I had not told my friend that the Lord had put in my heart the desire for creating some food production innovations. I was recalling some of the ideas I had been throwing around in my head for the last several months when suddenly a strikingly Herculean-sized guy thumps me in the chest with his massive finger and says, "I hate you guys!!"

In that moment of unexpected somewhat aggressive confrontation, I didn't know if I should fight or run! His angry comment was so out of place for where we were. Then I realized he was a bit tipsy and being at least two heads taller than me, I didn't want to provoke him, so I let him talk. He repeated himself saying, "Yeah, I hate you guys! You're always trying to think up a new way to lower the detection limit of an atomic absorption spectrophotometer!" That got my attention because that's the instrument I worked with in the laboratory!

He continued, "Do you know who I am?" But without waiting for a response, he continued, "I am . . . (and he mumbled his name that I didn't catch); with my first invention I received 27 patents! All the fruit trees in Southern California are sprayed from my patents!" Still poking my chest, he shot back loudly, "Why don't you guys put your minds to good use and come up with new ways of food production or preservation?" Without another word, he walked off, and I found myself choked up because he spoke about the very things that the Lord had put in my heart to do! Could it be the Lord was using an obnoxious burly bully to make a point by poking me directly in my heart as he spoke?

As I was still mentally jarred from what had just happened, my friend came up to me and said, "I think these venture capital guys will be talking all night, and we have work tomorrow." Checking my watch, I saw it was 11 PM, so I nodded in agreement, and we headed out the front door of the now-closed COSI building. It was a clear, crisp autumn evening, and the well-lit sidewalk was empty except for this little black beggar guy standing by the street.

He looked pretty ragged like he had been living on the streets for a long time. As he started walking towards us, I began fishing around in my pocket for some money to give him. Coming up to me, he asked, "Do you think I can get a job in there?", referring to the COSI building behind me.

I pointed up at the glass front of the building to a second-floor office and advised, "If you go up there tomorrow during business hours, they can tell you if any jobs are available."

Deftly, he moved in closer and got his face just inches away from my face, and that's when I was completely awed by his brilliant, penetrating blue eyes! Sticking his finger in my face, he declared in a very clear and strong voice, "It's time to just Praise the LORD!" Instantly, I knew he was referring to the food innovations the Lord had put on my heart that the big guy kept thumping.

Before I had a chance to say anything, the little beggar stepped behind me, and I turned to question him, but he was gone! There were wall-to-wall closed buildings behind me for a long downtown block and the open street in front of me; there was nowhere he could have gone in those seconds where I wouldn't have been able to see him.

I looked at my friend and voiced, "Where did he go?", to which he replied with wide eyes and a puzzled look, "I have no idea" as he slowly shook his head.

My friend left, and I went to my car that was parked nearby. Closing the door behind me, rather than turning on the ignition to head home, I just sat there to reflect on what had just transpired. I was so astounded by the beggar's words, his stunning blue eyes and the realization that he was so much more than he appeared to be—I had no doubt the LORD had just sent an angel to deliver a message directly to me. A message that could not have been any more clear: It was an unquestionable affirmation that my cluster of food innovation ideas were not just some rambling thoughts, but were concepts the LORD had placed in my mind and heart—thoughts that I needed to pay attention to. He sent an angel to lock them in place in my heart, to let me know I needed to be creative in that direction.

As I pondered the significance of these events that had just happened, my car became a holy sanctuary in the presence of the LORD, and my heart became overcome with emotion; I could do nothing but gladly embrace the moment, weeping as my spirit aligned with His will. I was completely undone before the Master Inventor.

There is no way to describe in mere words the impact of that late-night God-orchestrated rendezvous; it remains incredibly vivid in my mind to this day. It's true I didn't completely understand then, but I can tell you that Holy Spirit-engineered God encounters are not easily forgotten—ever.

And to be honest, I still don't completely understand, especially given the fact that to date, I have not come up with any food innovations that would warrant an angelic visitation. However, like my Uncle Paul, I don't care if anyone believes me or not—I was there, and I know that I know that I know what I experienced. Over the years I have come to understand more clearly that God has his own timing regarding the details of our lives—details that make complete sense to Him, which, in turn, become opportunities for us to trust our unknown futures to Him ....with hearts that are only fixed on Him. In time, He will bring all things about and all will become clear.

I fully expect to see that blue-eyed "beggar" again—the next time on his home turf in heaven—and I'll greet him with a heartfelt and hardy

"Thank you!" for delivering his, "It's time to just Praise the LORD" message that has long stayed very close to my heart.

> "All things were created through Him, and apart from Him not one thing was created that has been created." John 1:3 (HCSB)

Our God is still in the design business, and I'm staying tuned, waiting for the next step.

ANGEL #3

Terry and I are friends, and we go way back; we are old guys now and "way back" means we were diaper buddies! So, you might say I know Terry pretty well. Not only do I believe his story, but I also have some insight into his life.

Still struggling with some old issues in his life, he was in deep turmoil and kept asking God why the bad things that happened to him in life happened. Wrestling with these things had also taken a toll on his body, both physically and emotionally.

Internally, things had gotten so bad he felt like his life had no value and no future; he was just barely existing day after long day.

Then one day while in his driveway cleaning out the back of his car, he pulls his head out of the back seat, standing up to give his back a rest, and he notices a woman standing on the sidewalk near his house.

Living in a nice suburb of Las Vegas, he knew his neighbors, and he knew he had never seen this woman before, so he assumed she was a relative or friend visiting one of his neighbors. Being the only other person outside on the warm, sunny day besides himself, he couldn't miss seeing her.

Appearing to be a nice-looking woman in her early 30s, she proceeded to walk to Terry who was still next to his car, and instead of the normal, "Hello" one might expect, she questioned, "Do you believe in Jesus?" Terry thought that was pretty odd but responded, "Yes!"

As she stepped in closer, Terry instantly felt peaceful and knew that everything that was happening was supposed to happen. Then she requested, "Can I pray for you?" Living and ministering in Las Vegas, Terry is very reluctant to have a total stranger pray for him because of previous encounters with bizarre and weird, cult-type people.

But surprisingly, because of how everything felt so right, he found himself saying, "Yes!"

She reached across with her right hand and took his right hand in hers and held it as she started to pray. Immediately, Terry felt like she knew him and knew his future. Even more profoundly, he no longer felt like his life was useless and of no value; in an instant, he now had a future filled with hope! He was overwhelmed by a sense of wellness and peace, which he hadn't felt for years.

He was also amazed at how soft her hand was; in fact, it was the softest hand he had ever held in his life. With Terry being an artsy guy and an accomplished musician, he is more aware than most about his surroundings and feelings and the contrast of things.

The truth is that he was quite distracted by how unearthly soft her hand was that he wasn't listening closely to her prayer, but he was aware that she was praying about his future. When she finished, Terry recounted that the smile she smiled at him was a beautiful smile that just didn't quit!

As she backed away, Terry voiced, "God bless you!"

As beautiful as her smile was the first time, he expressed that her smile the second time was completely indescribable—it was heavenly, a smile and face he will never forget. Ever!

She walked behind his car to leave, and Terry stuck his head back in his car to continue cleaning, mulling over what had just happened. In no more than a minute, he pulled his head out again, curious to see where she was walking to, but she was gone!

Terry lives on a straight street, and there is nowhere she could have gone out of his sight in that minute. He walked down his driveway to the sidewalk to look further down into the neighborhood, a very open area, but . . . no sight of her.

Walking back into his house, as he stepped into the kitchen, the first thing his wife Donna noticed was the peace that emanated from his face that she hadn't seen in years.

Terry started, "Donna, you'll never believe what just happened to me!"

Before she could even catch herself, the Holy Spirit flowed out of her, "You met an angel!"

And indeed, Terry had.

<<>>

The previous bonus story was taken from the book below.

To see the book below and Nick's other books go to: AuthorNick.com[1]

<<>>

---

1. https://authornick.com/

UNEXPECTED
GOD
ENCOUNTERS
A Collection of True Stories
NICK NICHOLS

The Thing Behind the Curtain

<<>>

Snowflakes drifted past the glowing streetlights, gently falling to the soft, fluffy white blanket of snow covering the frozen ground. It was a perfect evening for caroling. At ten years old, I could hardly wait for Christmas to arrive—not only the gifts but also our traditional Christmas caroling created even more anticipation of the holiday.

Every year a group of folks from our church would drive around the neighborhoods and sing carols to the elderly folks from our church who had a hard time getting out; it was a festive way to spread Christmas cheer, bring a smile to their faces and lift their spirits!

When our group arrived at a home, after piling out of the cars, my friends and I always managed a quick snowball fight before the singing started. At some homes, we were invited in while at other homes, we would try to read our caroling booklet under the dim porch light while the old folks would stand smiling by their open door, sometimes joining us in singing the old familiar tunes.

And often these old folks were ready for us! When the singing stopped, out came the cookies!! Instantly turning a chunky kid like me into all smiles! I loved the caroling and the cookies or maybe it was the other way around—the cookies and the caroling! But of all the old folks we went to sing to, there was one home I dreaded going to.

Old Mrs. Trimble's home scared the willies out of me! She lived in an older section of town where we climbed up the crumbling concrete steps from the street to her side of an old duplex. Every year, for the last two years in my short kid memory, she had invited us inside, and she never gave cookies.

The house smelled old, with old wood and paint, and it always had the weird mix of nursing home and ointment smells mixed in. But the worst part was the solid black curtain, behind which was—the Thing. As we entered, the Thing made groaning noises, short grunts, and screams, and you'd hear it banging around like an animal in a cage.

Everyone seemed to be ignoring this, like it was normal, but not me! I was terrified! Mrs. Trimble's living room was long, narrow and dimly lit; she would always sit in the back in a large chair, which caused all of us carolers to have to stand right beside the black curtain at the opposite end of the room by the front door. This time as we all crowded in, I was forced to the back of the group and right against the curtain next to "the Thing."

The caroling started and the Thing got more noisy and active—only the curtain stood between me and the Thing. I was always a very curious kid, and so, as scared as I was, my curiosity got the best of me, and I decided to gather up my courage and get a look at the Thing. When the moment was right while everyone was heartily singing, I slipped behind the black curtain.

At first, all I saw was the end of what looked like a big baby bed with its sides pulled up to keep the baby from falling out. Slowly walking around to the side of the bed, I stepped back shocked as the Thing came into full view—it shrieked, and I nearly wet my pants! But my curiosity kept me riveted in place.

The Thing had the twisted up body of a teenage girl!! Her legs and arms were twisted at unnatural pretzel-like angles, forcing her face down right against the mattress, and she was looking right at me!!!! She made a low growling noise as foamy saliva drooled out of her mouth, puddling on the mattress. The wild look in her eyes was unnerving, and I stepped back further while the carols continued on the other side of the curtain.

I had never seen anything like this, and I was afraid at any moment she would leap out of the bed and attack me! Fascination and fear gripped me like a vice, but my eyes were locked on hers. Then to my complete amazement, in an odd sort of way, she smiled at me!

At that moment, I was no longer afraid, but completely confused as my ten-year-old little brain couldn't process this at all! As I quickly moved back out to the other side of the curtain, she made some more grunts and shrieks and for a moment, it seemed like she was calling for me to come back. Slipping back into the group of carolers as they finished their last song, we waved goodbye to old Mrs. Trimble and left.

I didn't tell anybody anything, not even my closest friends, except I did tell my cousin Jo who was like my sister about my moment with the Thing, or rather the girl, and what I had seen and experienced. It scared her too, because she had heard the Thing moaning and screaming during the caroling.

Over the years, as I grew older, I learned "the Thing" was old Mrs. Trimble's daughter who was born with multiple severe birth defects. She happened to be the younger sister of a lady I really respected in our church named Mary Ann and the Thing was the aunt to Mary Ann's sons, my friends Dan and Terry.

On the rare occasion when old Mrs. Trimble would come to church, she would sit in the back, and when the preacher said something that touched her heart, she would shout out, "Amen, Brother!! Preach it!!" And even more rarely, she would bring her daughter in a kind of large mobile bassinet, and would park her in the aisle where her daughter squealed and grunted through the service.

One of the things I really started to admire about old Mrs. Trimble was she didn't care anymore what people thought about her or her daughter! She had gotten past all that shallow surface junk. She just loved her Jesus and loved her daughter, and everyone knew it. She, along with her daughter, had actually become an inspiration to me to do what Jesus had put in my heart to do, and not worry about what people thought of me.

Now that I'm an old guy, I understand completely what was really going on when I met old Mrs. Trimble's deformed daughter. When I slipped behind that curtain as a kid, I had really stepped into a love story—the love of a mother for her daughter that was so great Mrs. Trimble refused to have her daughter institutionalized but made the decision to care for her as long as she was able. It was love upon love and total commitment.

I have since prayed that the Lord would give me the same love for my family as old Mrs. Trimble had for her daughter—the same unconditional love that Jesus has for us!

After I'm dead and gone, I fully expect to be strolling along the streets of gold in Heaven and be tapped on the shoulder—turning, I'll see a stunningly beautiful woman, whose eyes spark recognition that tugs at a long-ago memory. She steps back, and with a graceful flourish, stretches her arms out wide, and with a glowing smile says, "Do you remember me?"

"I was the twisted up 'Thing,' and look at me now!

Jesus, yes, my wonderful Lord Jesus...has made me whole."

<<>>

"He will wipe every tear from their eyes. There will be no more death or mourning or crying or pain, for the old order of things has passed away."
—Rev. 21:4 NIV

<<>>

The previous bonus story was taken from the book below.

To see the book below and Nick's other books go to: AuthorNick.com[1]

<<>>

---

1. https://authornick.com/

A COLLECTION OF TRUE STORIES
Spiritual Lessons
THAT CHANGED MY LIFE
Nick Nichols

Bankrupt . . . but Blessed!

< < > >

Laughing around our dinner table, my wife and I, and our four young children heard the knock at the door. Taking the stairs down to the front door in our split-level home and flipping on the porch light, I opened the door. There stood a tall man complete with a holstered gun, black nightstick, handcuffs attached to his belt, and a black jacket that said in bright yellow letters—SHERIFF.

Inviting him into the entryway, I said, "How can I help you?" But my heart sank; I knew why he was there.

"I'm here to serve you a subpoena; you need to appear in court, and the bank will be taking your home." I was stunned by his blunt statement, then immediately dropped my head shaking it back and forth. This visit was not totally unexpected, but hearing those harsh words certainly brought the reality of it out into the open.

Though he was just the messenger, in the humiliation of the moment, I found myself trying to explain how we had come to this point. After listening politely, he responded, "You seem like a nice guy, and I'm really sorry to have to serve you this subpoena." Thanking him for doing his job, I offered him some dinner, which he declined, and he was off into the night. Our dream home, the home we had prayed for, the home we had built, was now going back to the bank, and we would be out on the street, or so I felt.

Five years before, in 1987, everything looked bright, and my wife and I were a little fearful but optimistic as I struck out on my own as an Environmental Consultant. I believed this was the direction the Lord wanted me to take, and so I did. The average hourly wage at that time was about $9 an hour. The first year I charged $25 an hour and found work. The second year I charged $50 an hour, and no companies complained. The third year I charged $75 an hour and still no reaction. So, the fourth year, I charged $100 an hour.

One afternoon the CEO of a large national company took me out for lunch and said, "You know, Nick, you could have been charging us $100 an hour four years ago, and we would have happily paid it because we saw you as cheap insurance to stand between us and all the confusing regulatory requirements of the Environmental Protection Agency!"

As I began to realize my worth in the marketplace, I became more fixated on making money, and my relationship with the Lord began to drift into the background. Down in my heart of hearts, I knew I was off track and going downhill spiritually. Somewhere in there, I prayed in a meager mumble, "Lord help me to be focused on you and not on myself and my skills."

The answer to that prayer came with the recession of the early 1990s. In consulting, I was spending half my time helping companies unravel the complexities of federal environmental regulations and the other half of my time doing custom fabrication or repairs for non-commercial research laboratories and private industry. My standard practice was to put all the costs of a fabrication or repair job on a credit card. My billing cycle was every 30 days, so I could buy the materials, do the job, and pay off the card each month after the company paid me, and I would then keep the difference.

But as the recession set in, companies started pulling in their purse strings, and ALL my clients started paying me 60, 90, 120 days out or not at all! Some companies I had contracts with were very large, and they knew it would cost me more to go after my money than what they owed.

As the recession deepened, nobody was contracting the services I offered. This launched me into using credit cards for the essentials of living—buying food and paying utilities—and turned into the vicious cycle of using one credit card to pay another. Soon, I was in over my head, and in answer to my meager-mumbled prayer, it wasn't long before I was on my knees praying for help, and my focus turned back to the Lord.

As our debt increased, we began receiving calls from credit collection agencies. Every time they called, I would try to explain our situation and offer partial payment, but they would have none of it—"Pay the full amount, or we'll ruin your credit," they threatened. Some even started swearing at me on the phone and would call at all hours of the day and night, so I felt I had to resort to using an answering machine to screen the calls before answering.

Dealing with the creditor phone calls was certainly annoying, but it went to a whole new level when the neighbors started coming to me saying they had received a strange call asking if we still lived in our house, or if I still had my car and other such questions. The creditors were trying to see what assets I still had—and generally, harass me via my neighbors! And, yes, the creditors knew exactly what they were doing since everyone knows how embarrassing it is having your neighbors know you're sinking financially.

When I didn't think it could get any worse, it did . . . when I received notification in the mail that I was being sued by TWO companies! One of them was one of the largest and most prestigious law firms in our large city. I tried to negotiate with them, but again, no deal, and against my desire, they forced me into bankruptcy!! The last thing I ever wanted—but now, I had no choice. My wife and I were devastated, and we were so out of money that I couldn't even afford a bankruptcy attorney.

Needing to respond to the lawsuits, I went to our state Supreme Court law library and started digging into bankruptcy law. After days of digging, I discovered bankruptcy law was a massive pile of convoluted information with no clear direction—at least none that I could find.

One day standing between two large shelves of law books and in complete despair, in desperation I prayed, "Lord, I know this is all my fault from when I turned my focus from You to money, but I know you have forgiven me, and right now I need help and guidance about filing bankruptcy—I REALLY need help! In the name of Jesus, Amen." Still standing and despairing and staring at the floor, I noticed a skinny binder in line with the toe of my shoe.

Pulling out the small, thin binder, I flipped it open and almost fell over with shock—it was a continuing education course for attorneys who wanted to start practicing bankruptcy law!! It said, "#1. Tell your client to..., #2. Then file this for your client," and so on. It was a step-by-step guide of how attorneys should take their clients through bankruptcy! I bowed my head and said, "Thank you, Lord, for this awesome instant answer to prayer!! I know I don't deserve it but thank you so much!" I started following the guide and later found other useful legal self-help books.

As time went on, and as I kept studying and filing documents with the court, a date was eventually set for a court appearance. This had been a long and involved process; from the time the sheriff showed up at our door to this point had taken over two years—two years that we miraculously got to stay in our house! Before the court date, I filed a half-page brief with the court regarding a new bankruptcy ruling by the United States Supreme Court that I believed applied to my situation. The law firm suing me responded with a 32-page rebuttal!!

My day in court finally came, and it was intimidating. The courtroom was a large room with a very high ceiling; there were two old wooden podiums ten feet apart, one for me, and one for the opposing attorney. About thirty people sat behind us, and there was a large gulf of deep red carpet that dipped down several steps from us to the judge on the distant opposite side of the room and then back up a few steps to his bench. The judge sat in a throne-like wooden chair at a mammoth wooden bench that was surrounded by a very ornate wood railing. As I said, it was intimidating.

Looking beside me at the trim and fit law firm attorney in his $1,000 suit, I watched as he tamped and evened his handful of documents, ignoring me like I was a worthless piece of smelly street rubbish from the alley behind the courtroom. He was getting ready to go for the jugular—my jugular!! The judge looked at me and said, "Son, what is your stand on this bankruptcy issue?" I read my half-page document and then waited.

The judge then turned his attention to the confident, arrogant attorney who was just opening his mouth to speak, but before he could get a word out, the judge held up his hand for him to be silent and said, "Counselor, are you aware that the decision you based your entire argument on in this case was rescinded yesterday by the U.S. Supreme Court?"

The attorney looked stunned . . . and totally speechless. For a few moments, he looked like a deer caught in the headlights of an oncoming car. Trying to recover, he started rapidly tamping his wad of documents and then said, "But your honor, there are still the merits of the case to be considered!" The judge ignored him.

Looking back at me, the judge said, "Son, you have chosen one of the most highly contested issues in bankruptcy law; why, I don't even know what I think about it!"

Then with the crack of the gavel, the judge declared, "Case dismissed!" That was over thirty years ago. I was not sued; the bank did take our house, but with the Lord's help we were able to find a townhouse apartment that accepted a family of six.

Over time, the Lord restored everything to us including another house, but most important of all, the Lord restored my focus on Him!!

Yes, bankrupt . . . *but blessed!*

<<>>

"For the LORD will be your confidence and will keep your foot from being caught." —Proverbs 3:26 (KJV)

<<>>

The previous bonus story was taken from the book below.

To see the book below and Nick's other books go to: AuthorNick.com[1]

---

1. https://authornick.com/

<<>>

><>:<><

If you've read the sample stories from my spiritual books and want to have a relationship with Jesus, then here's how—

"If you want this light and love in your life, say a prayer like this—whether for the first time or to express again your passionate desire to follow Jesus:

Jesus, you are the light of the world. I want to follow you, passionately and wholeheartedly. But my sins have separated me from you. Thank you for your love for me. Thank you for paying the price for my sins, and I trust your finished work on the cross for my rescue.

I turn away from the thoughts and deeds that have separated me from you. Forgive me and awaken me to love you with all my heart, mind, soul, and strength. I believe God raised you from the dead, and I want that new life to flow through me each day and for eternity.

God, I give you my life. Now fill me with your Spirit so that my life will honor you and I can fulfill your purpose for me. Amen.

You can be assured that what Jesus said about those who choose to follow him is true: "If you embrace my message and believe in the One who sent me, you will never face condemnation, for in me, you have already passed from the realm of death into the realm of eternal life!" (John 5:24).

But there's more! Not only are you declared "not guilty" by God because of Jesus, you are also considered his most intimate friend (John 15:15). As you grow in your relationship with Jesus, continue to read the Bible, communicate with God through prayer, spend time with others who follow Jesus, and live out your faith daily and passionately. God bless you!"

Quote taken from the The Passion Translation

https://www.thepassiontranslation.com/

If you prayed the above prayer, I suggest you start reading the Gospel of John.

I prayed this type of prayer on February 2, 1971, and Jesus changed my life—forever!!

Blessings!

Nick Nichols

><>:<><

Professor Polly the Parrot

<<<>>>

Pulling me aside, the pet shop manager had an angry look on his face.

Poking his finger in my face he started in, "If that parrot says to a customer what you're teaching him to say—YOUR FIRED!" He punctuated that with a finger thump to my chest and a few choice curse words about me and the parrot!

That meant only one thing to me, I had to buy the expensive parrot and take it home for job security!

It all started simply enough when I got a job through my buddy Norm at a pet store while in high school in the early '70s. It was a crappy job, because that's what I was hired to do, clean the poop out of cages. Butt, being a critter fan, it wasn't all bad.

We had adorable puppies to play with, kittens, multiple kinds of birds, aquariums with colorful fish, lizards, snakes, hermit crabs, hamsters, mice, and occasionally exotic animals. Squirrel Monkeys were my favorite, we'd get around five of them in at a time and put them in a large cage. I'd put on a big long leather welding glove to feed them because as soon I put my hand in the cage, they would grab the food, bite my gloved hand, pee on me, poop on me, and scream at me! Eventually they calmed down, became less aggressive, and were fun to watch.

Another time we got a colorful bird called a Toucan that was popular at the time because of the Toucan that was on front of the Fruit Loops cereal box. That guy was beautiful till he ate, he would sling food everywhere. He was fun to watch eat . . . at a distance!

The fish we had were your basic Tetras, Guppies, and Gold Fish, etc, and once the manager ordered some Piranhas. Theodore Roosevelt in 1913 during his travels along the Amazon River in Brazil wrote in his best seller, "Through the Brazilian Wilderness," a great description about Piranhas...

"They are the most ferocious fish in the world. Even the most formidable fish, the sharks or the barracudas, usually attack things smaller than themselves. But the piranhas habitually attack things much larger than themselves. They will snap a finger off a hand incautiously trailed in the water; they mutilate swimmers—in every river town in Paraguay there are men who have been thus mutilated; they will rend and devour alive any wounded man or beast; for blood in the water excites them to madness. They will tear wounded wild fowl to pieces; and bite off the tails of big fish as they grow exhausted when fighting after being hooked." Later he witnessed a pack of Piranhas attacking and devouring an entire cow.

Those were the guys we had in our tank! Fortunately they were little guys about the size of a silver dollar. The big ones could get up to fourteen inches long, with a body about the size of my shoe. Anyway, one day a customer came in and wanted to buy a Piranha. Being the first time for me to deal with them I carefully netted the one he wanted and flipped him out of the net into my ready plastic bag of water.

Grabbing the top of the bag I gave it a quick twist trapping lots of air in the half full bag. After knotting the bag I was handing it to the customer when suddenly all the water poured out of the bag and the customer and I looked down seeing the Piranha flopping around on the floor. Grabbing my net I scooped him up and plopped him back in the tank were he went back to swimming like normal. Holding up the bag, we saw he had bitten a large chunk out of the side of the bag leaving a surgically cut scalloped hole!

After that, I was very, very, careful netting the Piranhas for customers. However, most of the time I didn't work out front with the customers, but worked in the back cleaning cages. That's were the problem started with the bird. We had a Red Fronted Amazon parrot covered with mostly vivid green feathers and a bright patch of red on it's forehead with some light blue feathers behind that.

She also had some yellow on her cheeks with some additional touches of red on her wings. She stood about a foot tall with a seventeen inch wing span, so she was a sizable parrot with a light colored beak and strong bite. Her previous owner had named her Polly, and Polly was an outstanding talker!

Being a parrot fan but never having owned one, I took a broom handle and stuck it between two wooden cage supports and would set Polly on it and talk to her while I was cleaning cages. She'd say things like, "Polly wants a cracker!" "Polly's a pretty bird." "Hey handsome!" "Hello!" "Bye, bye!" and other random phrases would occasionally pop out of her.

After a couple of weeks of this, and to vary her vocabulary, I thought it would be funny to teach her to say, "I'm a green son of a bi_ch!" I started working on her till the day the store manager walked in and heard me!!

After threatening me with being fired if Polly ever said that to a customer I asked the manager if I could buy the bird. He responded, "Fifty bucks and she's yours." At the time, that was two weeks of my pay! As I mentioned before it was an investment in job security so I bought her and took her home.

Polly got mixed reviews out of my parents who were willing to buy her a big cage which saved me another week's pay. The only place we found to put her that would keep her around us through the day, since she was a sociable bird, was in our kitchen by the window so she would see us and could look outside into our backyard.

My dad liked her right off, but she didn't like him! Like most parrots, Polly tended to be a one person bird. With all the time we'd spent together at the pet store, Polly and I had bonded. She would put her head down for me to scratch, but the moment my dad tried, she would threaten him with a screech and open-beak ready for attack!! It took awhile for her to warm up a bit to my mom, and for my mom to warm up to her too, eventually they got along OK but nothing like Polly and I.

As time went on, we would leave her door open and she would climb out on top of her cage and sit on a piece of wood we had up there. One of my dad's favorite things to do was when I would come into the kitchen, he'd run over to me and begin rapidly patting me on the shoulder and Polly, trying to protect me, would fly off her cage in a rage and dive bomb my dad trying to attack him.

Still with some agitation she would settle down on my shoulder and occasionally nip my ear because she was still railed up from my dad patting me. I belonged to her and she made that abundantly clear—and here I thought I owned her. Ha!

Eventually my dad did score some points with Polly. My dad loved Coca Cola and drank it every day and one time he was curious, and as I watched, he took a spoonful of Coca Cola over to Polly. She screeched at him as he inched forward with the spoon. With a sudden lunge she bit the spoon spilling the coke on the floor. My dad recoiled yanking the spoon back and she drew back into her fighting stance, only with a funny look on her face. She had inadvertently gotten a taste of Coca Cola.

My dad and I looked at each other, like, did she like it? He got another spoonful and inching closer she started screeching and screaming again, till he got within beak reach when she abruptly shut up and drank it! Then she leaned back, lifting one foot in the air while balanced on the other, she spread out one wing behind her raised foot while bobbing up and down making freaky chirping noises with her pupils dilating in and out from large to small! We took that as a, YES, she liked it!

From then on, the only way my dad could get close to her was with a spoon full of Coca Cola. Even then she would give him the evil eye, like that's close enough buddy! Forcing him to hold the spoon out at arms length. Then after downing her spoonful she would do her eye-dilating Coca Cola I-like-it dance!

After a while Polly got to the point of flying from her cage top to the kitchen table where my dad was sitting as soon as she would hear him crack open a cold coke. Which got to be annoying for my dad since she still wouldn't let him scratch her head without going for his finger. My dad started a no scratch—no coke policy, and that ended Polly's drinking days.

Speaking of my dad, he had to go to the hospital one time for some minor surgery and I drove over by myself to the hospital to visit him. After parking, I made my way to the first floor elevator to go up to his room on the sixth floor. On the second floor the hospital elevator doors opened and on stepped a pretty young nurse. She glanced at me and smiled; then she glanced at me a couple more times and her smile continued growing. Thinking to myself—"Hmm . . . is it my smile she likes? Or, maybe she likes my new cool woodsy outdoor jacket?"

I was getting ready to say something to her when the doors opened again and off she went . . . glancing back at me one more time grinning from ear to ear, and the doors shut. A few more floors up, I got off the elevator to go see my dad who'd just had recently come out of surgery. Walking into his room, and after greeting him with a quick, "Hi, Pop," he looks up at me and starts laughing. I'm thinking he must still be under the influence of the anesthesia.

Pointing at my cool jacket, he said, "What's that?"

Looking down, I saw I had this huge gob of creamy white and green parrot poop on my shoulder stretching halfway down the front of my jacket!! Obviously, it wasn't my smile or cool jacket that had the cute nurse grinning...thanks to Polly who had been sitting on my shoulder before I left for the hospital. Since Polly was a good-sized parrot, she'd dropped on me a good-sized load!

One thing Polly loved was to be set outside the kitchen in her cage to more clearly see the other birds instead of looking through the kitchen window plus she enjoyed the breeze. Coming in from our backyard garden one time my dad said, "Why don't we put her up in the tree and she can be with the other birds?" That sounded good to me so he threw a rope up into the tree and over a branch and fished the short end back to the ground tying it to the handle on top of her cage.

Pulling on the other end of the rope I hoisted her up into the tree and tied the end around the tree trunk. Polly was about twenty feet off the ground surrounded by leaves and birds. She seemed thrilled to be up there! One of the funny things while in the tree she often imitated the other birds she was hearing which left them really confused like something wasn't right with what they were seeing and hearing.

During the summer that became a regular thing, my dad or I would hoist Polly up in the tree where she would talk away or mimic the other birds, or loudly happy-screech! Frequently there were neighbor kids that would come around freely walking into our open backyard looking up in the tree watching and talking to Polly. The kids loved her, even the neighbors liked her and would put up with her occasional happy screeches.

One Saturday we heard a light tapping at our back door. Looking through the screen door I didn't see anybody because the bottom half of the door was a solid metal panel. Opening the door I nearly knocked over this petite, tiny, little girl! Looking up at me with great concern she shyly voiced, "Where's Polly?"

"Where's Polly? I repeated! I thought to myself, she's up in the tree, where else would Polly be. Walking out in the backyard I saw some other kids staring up in the tree, and looking up, there was Polly's cage door hanging open and no Polly!!

I told the kids, "Quick! Scatter and see if you can find Polly!" Running inside I told my parents and we each grabbed a handful of peanuts in the shell. Polly liked peanuts way more than crackers. My mom went out the front door turning left, my dad went right, and I ran across the street to look in the other neighbor's open backyards. We're all yelling her name, and we walked around for about an hour trying to find her.

Returning back to the street I saw a neighbor waving at me from about ten houses down. While running towards him he yelled, "We heard this screeching out in our backyard tree that was scaring my wife and saw a parrot up there, I figured it must be yours!" I trotted on down to his house and sure enough in his backyard tree sat Polly clearly enjoying her great adventure.

Coaxing her out of the tree with a peanut, I got her safely into my arms and to the joy of the neighborhood kids and the relief of our neighbor's wife I carried Polly back to her cage. Somehow Polly had figured out how to open her door, so from then on we added a heavy metal wire twist to keep it shut when she was outside.

Most summers, while I was out of school, we'd take a two week vacation to either see my aunt and uncle who lived in Titusville, Florida, or out to Denver, Colorado to see my mom's favorite uncle. This summer would be a Colorado run. Polly was good about us leaving as long as we left her with plenty of food and water.

I quickly loaded up her cage with extra food and water, rinsed my hands off in the sink, and said goodbye to Polly. Rushing out the front door I jumped in to our packed running car and we were off! I loved seeing my relatives in Florida, but my mom's uncle Paul in Colorado was something else! He could play a squeeze box (a concertina), the harmonica, and spoons he'd rhythmically slap against his leg.

To top that off, he was an amazing storyteller!! I remember thinking as a child, if I could ever tell stories half as well as my great uncle Paul, I'd be a happy camper! Well, maybe someday.

The two weeks of fun, music, and story telling flashed by all too quickly and we were back in our driveway at home, pooped from the long drive from Denver. My first thought was, how's Polly. My dad passed me his keys and I unlocked the front door and jogged in to see Polly. She was standing like usual on her thick wood dowel in the middle of her cage looking well and healthy.

She looked at me and instead of saying, "Polly wants a cracker," or some other phrase when she was excited to see me she only said, "BLOOP." That was followed by bloop...bloop...bloop, in a short staccato succession.

I voiced with a grin, "Polly want a cracker!?"

She responded, "Bloop."

"Polly's a pretty bird!"

"Bloop."

"Hello!"

"Bloop"

I tried the big one, "Polly want a Coca Cola!?"

"Bloop...bloop...bloop."

My mom came in followed by my dad to also see how Polly was doing.

I offered, "Polly looks like she made it through the two weeks okay, but..."

"Bloop...bloop...bloop," rolled out of Polly.

My mom started laughing because it was a funny sound that we'd never heard her make before.

"Bloop...bloop."

My mom thought she heard something. Being a former traveling and record cutting singer in a Gospel trio, she had excellent hearing, so she told us to be quiet and stared at the floor, concentrating on listening.

She reacted, "Oh, my goodness!"

Walking over to the sink she heard the soft sound of bloop...bloop...bloop.

Looking up, she started laughing again stating, "Poor Polly!! She's been listening to the sink faucet dripping day and night for two weeks!! She's imitating the drip sound!"

Apparently in my rush to leave on vacation, I didn't get the sink faucet completely turned off! It took me a week of talking and playing with Polly to get her to say her old familiar phrases again. Still, years later, once in a while, out would pop a, "Bloop, bloop."

At this point, we'd had Polly for over twenty-five years! Red Fronted Amazons were known to live up to eighty years. I didn't know how old Polly was when I bought her, but whatever her age, add a quarter of a century and she was probably getting pretty old.

I say this because she was starting to get cranky! And since my dad had also been growing older he was starting to get a bit cranky too. But mainly at Polly who he had shared his beloved kitchen with for twenty-five years and now neither were being nice to the other.

It was obvious it was time for Polly to move to a new home. I was in a living situation where I couldn't take Polly. I asked a bunch of friends but they couldn't take her either, so sadly I put her up for sale describing her as a good talker. Within a couple of days I heard from a guy who raised parrots and he had been looking for a parrot that could talk and teach his young parrots to talk. I assured him she could talk up a storm and would make a great teacher!

Not long after, he came to pick her up. It made me feel better with him taking Polly as I watched his interaction with her. He was clearly a parrot guy! My mom and dad and I stood on the front porch watching as he and Polly backed out of our driveway.

In a way, it felt like Polly was graduating as we waved our final farewells to now—Professor Polly.

>> The End <<

<<>>

The previous bonus story was taken from the book below.

To see the book below and Nick's other books go to: AuthorNick.com[1]

<<>>

Critter Tales
Adventures With My Pet Pals
Nick Nichols

—Book Samples—

<<>>

92

Adventures of a Mall Santa

<<>>

Bursting into the photo lab David, the mall manager, said to me, "QUICK, put down what you're doing; our mall Santa cancelled, and we need a Santa NOW!!" On our way out the door he said, "I need you to be Santa for this week through Christmas Eve," and then almost as a second thought, he asked, "Have you ever been a Santa before?" I said, "No, and why ME??"

"You're big, you don't need pillows, you laugh a lot, and your eyes even kind of twinkle a bit," he said. I was dumb struck—thinking about myself as Santa!? The whole idea was so crazy and sudden that I burst out laughing with a "HO! HO! HO!!" to fit the moment —"SEE," he said, "That's what I mean; you'll make a GREAT Santa!!"

I thought about how getting roped into being Santa was an interesting twist from my regular life as a career chemist, a position I was giving up as my family and I were switching direction to head to Bangladesh to do economic development work through a mission organization. While we waited for all the details to fall into place, I decided this short-term job as a photo lab technician would fill the bill, not knowing that turning into an "instant" Santa was going to be part of the job description! However, in the excitement of the moment, I thought, "Sure, why not; how hard could it be?" As quickly as David had pulled me into this, just as quickly I decided I was up for the adventure! "Bring it on; where are my candy canes?"

David pushed me into a little changing room where several women helped me get into the Santa suit while another put on my beard and little glasses, another my hat and some rouge on my cheeks to give me the classic cherry-red cheeks that are a must for every Santa! There was a mirror hanging on the door, and I marveled at how quickly they transformed me from a lab tech into Santa Claus. I was so impressed I was half expecting Rudolph with his shiny red nose to show up at any moment with my sled!

Leaving the dressing room, we rushed to Santa's big fake-snow covered large sitting chair that had a huge picture of the North Pole for a backdrop and a little white picket fence surrounding the area covered with more fake-snow, glittering tinsel, and brightly colored Christmas presents that dotted the Styrofoam snow drifts inside the fence. All was lit up with colored Christmas lights and soft holiday music was playing in the background. Yep, the North Pole had descended to this Midwestern mall!

Lines were starting to form, and I had two hours to be Santa! Looking at the excitement on the little faces reminded me of how excited my children were when they went to see the mall Santa. All that got me smiling and waving at the kids and winking at a few moms, too, in good merriment! Yes, I could be Santa for two hours; I'd seen a million Santas in my lifetime, and I knew the game plan . . .

So with a little excitement mixed with a little fear and a little bewilderment from having never actually done this before, I saw there was no time for thinking about it anymore as a mother with her son in tow was heading right for me—"SANTA... you're on!"

[Story continues in book.]

<<>>

The previous bonus story was taken from the book below.

To see the book below and Nick's other books go to: AuthorNick.com[1]

<<>>

ADVENTURES
OF A
Mall
Santa
NICK NICHOLS

The Mystery of Grandpa's Christmas Cane

<<>>

Little Christian started climbing up into his Grandpa's lap, causing Grandpa to yank the big family Bible he had been reading out of the way. Sitting it on the stand by his walking cane, he and Christian jostled around in his big easy chair till they were both comfortable. Christian was ready to talk, and his Grandpa was always ready to listen.

"Grandpa?"

"Yes?"

"Why do you use a cane?"

<<>>

〈〈〉〉

Leaning back a bit, Grandpa said, "Well, as a young man I broke my foot in an accident, and it never healed quite right." Closing his eyes picturing the events, he said . . .

"My team of five climbers and I were halfway up Mount Everest, the highest mountain in the world, when a storm started blowing in. The sky had suddenly changed from a brilliant blue to a stormy gray. As the wind blew harder, the temperature dropped, and we found ourselves trapped by the storm on the side of the mountain.

"Yelling to my team through the howling wind, I told them we have to turn back and go back down the mountain. That's when my foot caught between two rocks, and at the same moment, the climber below me slipped on some loose ice on the side of the mountain, and . . ."

"Grandpa!"

"Once he fell, his safety rope jerked my entire body, breaking my trapped foot . . ."

"G-R-A-N-D-P-A!!"

Opening his eyes, Grandpa said, "What!?"

With a serious look, Christian said, "Tell me the truth, Grandpa!"

"Ok, a cow accidently stomped on my foot and broke it. Back on our farm when I was a few years older than you, one day when I was doing my chores, I was trying to get old Jughead into the stall to milk her, but something startled her real bad—she jumped back and smashed my foot. And it's just gotten worse over the years."

Christian beamed with delight catching Grandpa in one of his tall tales. Grandpa laughed and tosseled Christian's hair, thinking what a sharp little guy he was. He was always so full of questions, but the older Christian got, the harder it was for Grandpa to get Christian to believe his "creative" answers.

[Story continues in book.]

<<>>

The previous bonus story was taken from the book below.

To see the book below and Nick's other books go to: AuthorNick.com[1]

<<>>

---

1. https://authornick.com/

<<>>

Note: Photo attributions are listed in each book.

Don't miss out!

Visit the website below and you can sign up to receive emails whenever Nick Nichols publishes a new book. There's no charge and no obligation.

https://books2read.com/r/B-A-NVTG-ZOUVB

BOOKS 2 READ

Connecting independent readers to independent writers.

About the Author

During my 30-year career, I was a water quality chemist, environmental scientist, consultant, and technical writer. In my spare time, I worked on projects in aquaculture, hydroponics, aquaponics, bioremediation, and renewable energy. In addition, I have also been an adjunct instructor at two colleges teaching Cellular Biology and Business Math.

Now I am retired and writing this from an island in South East Asia where I live. My lovely wife has been with me for forty-eight years and we have four awesome adult children and three lovely children in Heaven.

--Nick Nichols

<<>>

Read more at https://authornick.com/.

www.ingramcontent.com/pod-product-compliance
Lightning Source LLC
Chambersburg PA
CBHW021016160726
47994CB00006B/2538